STORMCHASER

The Peril of Life Without God

The Peril of Life Without God

A Creative Study of the Book of Ecclesiastes

by Bryan Belknap

EMPOWERED™ Youth Products
Standard Publishing
Cincinnati, Ohio

CONTENTS

All Scripture quotations, unless otherwise indicated, are taken from the HOLY BIBLE, NEW INTERNATIONAL VERSION®. NIV®. Copyright © 1973, 1978, 1984 by International Bible Society. Used by permission of Zondervan Publishing House. All rights reserved.

Scripture quotations marked THE MESSAGE are taken from *The Message: The Wisdom Books.* Copyright © 1996 by Eugene H. Peterson. Used by permission of NavPress Publishing Group.

Edited by Dale Reeves and Leslie Durden
Cover and inside design by Dina Sorn

Copyright © 2000 by Standard Publishing
All rights reserved
EMPOWERED™ Youth Products is a trademark of Standard Publishing
Printed in the United States of America

Standard Publishing, Cincinnati, Ohio
A Division of Standex International Corporation

07 06 05 04 03 02 01 00
5 4 3 2 1

ISBN: 0-7847-1151-8

How to Use This Book — 7

Lesson 1
Chasing Shadows
Ecclesiastes 1 — 9

Lesson 2
Chasing Exhaustion
Ecclesiastes 2:1-11, 17-26 — 17

Lesson 3
Chasing Moments
Ecclesiastes 3:1-14; 4:1-12 — 25

Lesson 4
Chasing Satisfaction
Ecclesiastes 5 — 33

Lesson 5
Chasing Answers
Ecclesiastes 8:2-17; 9:11, 12 — 41

Lesson 6
Chasing God
Ecclesiastes 11:9–12:14 — 49

Bonus Session
This Is Your Life! — 57

How to Use This Book

Flying kites can get boring. I remember letting the kite out farther and farther until the string ran out. After watching my Tie-Fighter kite become a dot and float on the end of the string for a few minutes, I thought, *What now?*

Even today, I watch men with full-body kites wrestle with the wind. These high-tech kites require both hands and sometimes a harness to control a huge object that performs precipitous twists, turns and dead falls, much like the gravity-defying acrobatics of The Matrix. After hours of practice and perfection, though, these men have to ask the same question of their $195 kite as I did of my $1.95 one: *What now?*

Solomon, the wisest man in the history of the world, asked the same question. Looking back across the span of his life, his activities, his accomplishments and his kingdom, he made this earth-shattering statement: "That's it?!" If the richest, wisest, most powerful man in the world felt completely empty at the close of his life, what hope do the majority of us normal people have?

This question faces your students even now. Many hear that the teen years are the best that life has to offer. They look back across those years and sometimes remember only pain, insecurity, injustice, fear, heartbreak, acne and pop quizzes. Others see the end of high school as the end of fun, believing the rest of life to be a drudgery when compared to their "glory days." Still others move forward boldly, buying wholeheartedly into the "American Dream," pursuing career, fame and fortune at all costs. These achievers pour their lives into work and deeds that might delay their discovery of Solomon's truth, but they too will certainly come up empty in the end.

Stormchaser seeks to create a God-centered worldview for students to use the rest of their lives. The biggest decisions of their lives wait around the corner, especially choice of career and mate, and they need to look "above the sun" in order to find happiness in the horizontal life we have here on earth. There is more to this life, this "rat race" most Americans buy into, even though the world teaches us that this is the ultimate—the best life has to offer. King Solomon blows the lid off the lie, letting us know the best is lame. Only life with God truly satisfies.

This book should change your students' perspective from life "under the sun" to a life that looks "above the sun" for guidance and contentment. Students will identify the different paths in life that they can wander down and understand that each one ultimately leads to emptiness and futility, a "chasing after the wind." Finally, they will apply their knowledge to decision-making, especially concerning the "big decisions"—like career, where to go to school, marriage partner, hobbies and church involvement.

Each session in this book is divided into three sections: **Sighting the Storm, Entering the Eye** and **Living to Tell**. **Sighting the Storm** gets your students warmed up and into the Scripture for the week. **Entering the Eye** (this is when a person stands in the center of a storm) is the meat of the session, dealing with a theme or subject that involves deep discussion and dissection. Finally, the **Living to Tell** section wraps things up and gives students something they can take home and apply immediately. The goal for each session is not for it to be just a lesson to complete, but for it to become a way of life for your students. Each section contains two activities to choose from so you can tailor the session to fit your group's learning style and the particular needs of your students. In addition, each session ends with a midweek activity entitled **Calculating the Data**. This will reinforce each week's topic.

Since the media (especially music and film) make up a large part of students' identity and often shape their culture, we have included numerous **Check This!** suggestions in each session. These sidebars include music or movie clip suggestions, or skits that reinforce the teaching of the day. WARNING! Preview all film clips before using them. They are not always obviously "spiritual" or self-explanatory. Weave these illustrations into your presentation of the material. Without proper explanation before or after, they might become simply entertainment and not a powerful teaching tool. Also, there could possibly be offensive material before or after the suggested clip, so know when to start and stop it. I encourage you to use media whenever possible, because using students' culture and language is the best way to present them with truth. NOTE: The start points noted are from the opening studio logo of the movie, not the beginning of your tape. Reset the counter to 0:00:00 when the studio logo appears.

Two suggested resources, *Shock Wave* videos and *Sanctified Skits*, are available from Ground Zero Productions. You may call them at (310) 390-5611 or visit their web site at www.gbomb.com for more information on their videos, books and worship CD resources.

The book of Ecclesiastes speaks directly to students today, challenging them to pursue God as their central goal in life, as opposed to chasing after all kinds of other pursuits in the midst of the storm. As you prepare to address the storm warnings each week, ask God to help you reach your students with his pursuing love.

Groups with access to media will want to plan ahead to secure videos and order CDs. The United States Copyright Act treats displays or performance of multimedia presentations, films and videotapes by nonprofit organizations (including churches) to a small group of individuals as "public performances" even if no admission fee is charged. The fact that the church or one of its members may have purchased the copy of the film or videotape makes no difference. To avoid running afoul of the "public performance" prohibition in the Copyright Act, you must in each instance secure the copyright owner's permission or alternatively obtain an "umbrella license" from the Motion Picture Licensing Corporation.

To learn more about the umbrella license, contact the MPLC at 1-800-462-8855 or visit them on the web at www.mplc.com. You may also want to visit http://fairuse.stanford.edu/ for additional information on the Copyright Act and the "Fair Use Doctrine."

1 CHASING SHADOWS

A hit song by the band Creed asked, "What's this life for?" So many of your teens and their peers are asking the same thing. They look around and see only war and suffering and disease. Combine that with broken homes, violence, loneliness and the emptiness in materialism and it's easy to see why students are asking that question. Many believe themselves to be alone in a cruel world created by a God who doesn't care about them or understand.

As King Solomon neared the end of his days, he looked back over all he had experienced. He looked upon a world comparable to ours and asked similar questions. He saw the futility of life and sounded much like modern teens as they moan about the hand life has dealt them.

Thankfully, Solomon did come up with solid, biblically sound answers to his (and our) questions. We can learn from his life, not dooming ourselves to repeat his fruitless endeavors. Instead, your students will be ahead of the game, avoiding the traps that Solomon explored and entering into the abundant life Christ promised. This session will start students on their path to looking "above the sun" for meaning and answers to life.

As you begin this study, you might want to share some brief background information on Solomon and the book of Ecclesiastes. The book's title comes from the Greek word *ekklesia*, which roughly means "one who addresses an assembly." Solomon, the son of Bathsheba and David, wrote this very cynical book near the end of his life, after building the temple and helping Israel to become a wealthy world power. On top of this, he was the wisest man in the world, choosing wisdom when God offered to grant him any one request.

This session should introduce your students to Ecclesiastes and the thought that the pursuit of worldly things is empty and ultimately futile and unsatisfactory without God.

> **LESSON TEXT**
> Ecclesiastes 1
>
> **LESSON FOCUS**
> Life is meaningless without God.
>
> **LESSON GOALS**
> As a result of participating in this session, students will:
> - Understand that without God life is empty.
> - Realize there is nothing new in the world.
> - Learn exactly who Solomon was in history.

SIGHTING THE STORM

1 Fount of Wisdom

Begin this activity by asking students to line up from the youngest to the oldest. Students with the same age should line up by birthday. Once everyone is in line, have them sit down in birth order in straight rows, with the youngest in the first chair all the way to the oldest in the last chair.

Comment, **"Today is a special day. Each of you, with your various years of experience here on Earth as a baby, in elementary school and now in secondary school, has the opportunity to share your wealth of knowledge with your peers. Each of you will share one thing—hopefully the most important thing—you have learned in your life up to this point. We will hear from the youngest person first and finish with the oldest. Please be direct, sharing your advice in a sentence or two."**

Allow each student to come forward and share his or her "nugget" of wisdom. If you have a large group, you may want to put students in two or three lines and have them share their wisdom in smaller groups. Encourage everyone to speak, but do not force someone who does not want to. Students' comments will probably range from the spiritual to the silly, and that's fine. God teaches everyone in different ways and on different levels. After everyone has had an opportunity to share, say: **"Some of you might not feel like you've lived long enough to give 'life advice.' On the other hand, some of you may feel like you've packed 50 years into your life already. Either way, it is good to look back on your life and reflect on what you've learned. It's also smart to learn from your elders, people who have endured a great deal in their lifetimes."** Ask:

- Do you listen to the advice of your elders?
- Do you ever insist on trying something yourself even when warned of the danger? Why?

Conclude this activity by saying, **"At the end of his life, King Solomon, the wisest human being in history, wrote down what he had learned in the book of Ecclesiastes, which we're going to study for the next few weeks."** (Share whatever background information you feel necessary on either Solomon or Ecclesiastes that will help your students connect with today's study.)

2 The Wise Guy

Ahead of time, tear out of the newspaper or magazines photos of ten to twenty famous people. These people should range from the easily recognizable (movie stars, rock stars, sports figures, politicians) to the more obscure but equally important (scientists, theologians, authors, businessmen). These people should all be at the top of their professions, people with complete mastery of their jobs. One at a time, present all of the pictures to the entire group and see if students can identify each one. After all of the pictures have been shown to your students, say, **"Each of these men and women are specialists in their fields. They have extensive wisdom and knowledge in their specific subjects. There was one man in history, however, who possessed more wisdom than all these people put together. Does anyone know his name?"** (Wait for responses.) If no one says Solomon, reveal the answer, then ask: **"How did he become so wise?"**

Read aloud the account of Solomon receiving his wisdom in 1 Kings

Materials needed:
Ten to twenty pictures of various famous people; Bible

3:5-15. Fill in any extra information about Solomon or the book of Ecclesiastes that you feel will help them in the upcoming weeks. Then say, **"We're going to take the next few weeks to benefit from Solomon's wisdom and see what kind of advice he has for us today."**

ENTERING THE EYE

1. This Was Your Life

Distribute writing utensils and a copy of the reproducible student sheet on page 14 of this book to every student. Then explain: **"This is your obituary. Fill in the missing information with what you think it would say at the end of your life. Be honest, and be sure the information reflects 40, 60 or 80 years from now, rather than if you died today."**

Give students a few minutes to fill in their obituaries. Then ask them to break into groups of six to share what they wrote with their groups. They could divide themselves by the states in which they were born.

Let them discuss these questions in their groups:
- **Are you happy with what you wrote in your obituary?**
- **What can you do to change the things you dislike?**
- **What can you do to ensure that the things you like about what you wrote come true?**

Comment, **"I'm sure you have high expectations for your life. Everyone wants to make a difference. Assume that what you wrote comes true. Will your grandchildren remember? Will anyone outside your family remember? How long will your 'legacy' last?"**

Ask students to take turns reading aloud Ecclesiastes 1 to each other. Then, let them discuss these questions in their groups:
- **What does Solomon think of life?**
- **What are some of the things he lists as "meaningless"?**
- **Do you agree with Solomon? Why or why not?**
- **What things would you add to this list?**
- **What gives meaning to your life now?**
- **Will this meaningful thing carry you through the rest of your life?**

Materials needed:
Writing utensils; reproducible student sheet on page 14 of this book; Bibles

Check This . . .

To break the ice with humor, show a clip from the movie *Monty Python and the Holy Grail* that begins at 7:45 and lasts 1 1/2 minutes. The scene depicts a man trying to get rid of his grandfather who is not quite dead yet.

2. The Never-ending Story

Ask your students to break into groups of six and sit down in a circle. Then say, **"You are going to create a fairy tale. The first sentence is: 'Once upon a time there was a little girl.' The oldest person in the group will go first. He or she will add a sentence to continue the story. You will go around the circle five times, each person adding a new sentence to the story. The sentence you add can be as bizarre and crazy as you want it to be, sending the story in whatever direction you desire. But it must be**

Materials needed:
Bibles

connected to the sentence before it somehow. It can't be completely out of left field. When the story goes around the circle five times, raise your hands, and I will supply the last sentence to the story. Ready? 'Once upon a time there was a little girl. . . .'"

After each group finishes, complete its story with the sentence, **"She lived happily ever after in Fargo, running the Backstreet Boys' museum and caring for her ant farm."**

Ask students to discuss these questions:
- **Did the story make much sense?**
- **If your story had been a movie, what would you say about it after leaving the theater?**

Comment, **"We like to place meaning on the things we see and hear. It's important that they make sense. We try to do the same thing with everyday life—look at it and make sense of it. King Solomon looked at life and came to his own conclusion."**

Ask students to take turns reading aloud Ecclesiastes 1 to each other. Then, let them discuss these questions in their groups:
- **What is Solomon's theme here?**
- **How does it reflect the story you just created?**
- **How would you feel if your made-up story continued?**
- **Does life ever seem like that?**
- **What do you do to break up the monotony?**
- **Would God approve of your diversion?**
- **Will this diversion keep you entertained for your entire life?**
- **What gives your life meaning?**

Check This . . .

Play Sixpence None the Richer's song "Meaningless," from their album *The Fatherless and the Widow*.

Materials needed:
Butcher paper; masking tape; marker; Bibles

LIVING TO TELL

1 New and Improved

Tape a sheet of butcher paper on the wall where everyone can see it. Write: **"What has been will be again, what has been done will be done again; there is nothing new under the sun"** (Ecclesiastes 1:9) at the top of the sheet of butcher paper. Then ask students:
- **Who agrees with this statement?**
- **Who disagrees with it?**

Ask students to defend their answers. Then ask, **"Do we all agree that the Bible is the inspired Word of God?"** (This may prompt an important discussion about God's Word with students who do not agree. This is an important pillar of the Christian faith that you should cover now and continue discussing for the remainder of this session if necessary.)

Continue by saying, **"Let's make some lists together and figure out what Solomon is saying here about 'nothing' being new. What are some of the things you believe are new in the world?"**

On one side of the butcher paper, make a list of all the things that students feel are new in the world and unique from Solomon's day.

This list will probably include items like the telephone, TV, computer, cars, CDs, the U.S.A., cargo pants, etc. List as many as you feel appropriate and then stop taking answers.

Ask: **"Now, what are some of the things that are the same now as they were in Solomon's day?"**

On the other side of the butcher paper, make a list of your students' answers. They may have some difficulty here, but prompt them to create a list of answers like these: greed, war, love, selfishness, God, etc. After they finish with this list, break them into groups of four. In their groups, ask them to read Matthew 15:18-20, then answer the following questions:

- **Does new "stuff" make the heart of man different?**
- **Do you think human nature has changed since Solomon's time? Why or why not?**
- **Would Solomon say our society is different from his?**

Bring the whole group back together and look at the list of "new" things again. Say, **"Let's look at this first list again. Yes, these things are innovations and improvements, but are they really new, something the world has never seen before?"**

Go through the list and point out how Solomon's day had the same things, just in a more primitive form. In response to the list of examples given earlier, you would respond: communication—in the form of letters; entertainment—in the form of drama; transportation—in the form of a chariot; etc.

Conclude this activity by saying, **"Everything we have today is simply an advancement of what man had thousands of years ago. Solomon's words speak directly into our lives even with a generation gap larger than the Grand Canyon, because he speaks about human nature, and human nature without God does not change."**

2 Here Today, Forgotten Tomorrow

Distribute writing utensils and a copy of the reproducible student sheet on page 15 to every student. Ask students to fill it out the best that they can. When everyone is finished, give the correct answers to the test. They are as follows: *1b; 2h; 3j; 4g; 5c; 6i; 7d; 8e; 9a; 10f.*

Discuss these questions:
- **Did anyone get them all right?**
- **Could you have even come close if the names were missing?**
- **Would you consider any of these people famous now?**

Read Ecclesiastes 1:11 aloud. Then ask:
- **What does Solomon say happens to a man's work after he dies?**
- **Do you agree or disagree with this statement? Give an example to support your answer.**
- **Do the accomplishments by the people on your student sheet impress God?**
- **What mark are you trying to leave on the world?**
- **Will reaching your goal please God or impress men?**

Close by inviting students to pray for each other, asking for wisdom in making their goals pleasing to God and for discernment in changing temporal goals into eternal ones. Distribute the midweek devotional, **Calculating the Data,** and encourage students to complete the activity this week.

Materials needed:
Reproducible student sheets on pages 15, 16 of this book; writing utensils; Bibles

Check This . . .

Show the clip from the movie *Notting Hill* where Julia Roberts, Hugh Grant and friends sit around the dinner table and Julia talks about growing old and people thinking she looks like someone who was once famous. It begins at 42:30 and lasts until 43:45.

In Loving Memory

_____

died on _____ of _____.

He/she was born in _____, _____ on

_____, 19 ____ to Mr. and Mrs. _____. He/she will be

sorely missed by his/her siblings _____. Friends and family say

that he/she was a person of _____ who put

_____ first. Some of the ways that he/she made a difference include:

_____
_____
_____
_____.

Services will be held at noon tomorrow.

HERE TODAY
Forgotten Tomorrow

Draw an arrow from the correct name below to the corresponding achievement:

1. William Belknap
2. Mary Lou Retton
3. Dorothy Hodgkin
4. Ralph Nader
5. Edmund Rostand
6. Hudson Taylor
7. Norman Greenbaum
8. Barry Nelson
9. Frank Capra
10. Thomas Marshall

a. Directed the film *You Can't Take It with You*
b. President Grant's Secretary of War
c. Wrote *Cyrano de Bergerac*
d. Recorded the song, "Spirit in the Sky"
e. Played James Bond on TV in *Casino Royale*
f. Woodrow Wilson's Vice President
g. Safety guru
h. Won an Olympic gold medal
i. Missionary to China
j. Discovered vitamin B12

"All of us have become like one who is unclean, and all our righteous acts are like filthy rags" Isaiah 64:6.

Calculating The Data

"Am I now trying to win the approval of men, or of God? Or am I trying to please men? If I were still trying to please men, I would not be a servant of Christ" Galatians 1:10.

Apply this verse to all of your activities this week. Fill in every activity (school, sports, TV, phone, etc.) that you spend 30 minutes or more doing during the week. Then rate the permanence or meaninglessness of the activity on the chart below. Activities with eternal value score closer to the crown.

_____
_____
_____
_____
_____
_____
_____
_____
_____
_____
_____
_____
_____
_____

-5   -4   -3   -2   -1   0   1   2   3   4   5

How much eternal treasure are you stacking up in Heaven? Most of your activities are not without eternal purpose, but sometimes your focus is slightly off. For example, talking on the phone can bear tremendous fruit when you focus on building a friendship that ultimately leads the listener to Christ.

Redirect your focus on each of your activities so that it places God squarely in the middle of each activity. Look at this graph again in a week and see if you have moved any closer to the eternal goal, a crown of righteousness.

2 CHASING EXHAUSTION

"If it feels good, do it!" This seems to be the attitude of the entire world, not just young people these days. Every message from the media to scholars to friends tells students to indulge their every physical desire, again and again. This is not the attitude of Christ.

The apostle Paul said in 1 Corinthians 2:12: "We have not received the spirit of the world but the Spirit who is from God, that we may understand what God has freely given us."

Our spirit should be in conflict with the world. Cutting through all of the cultural crud is a difficult task. Solomon struggled with it thousands of years ago. He dove headfirst into the black lagoon of worldly muck and returned, still dripping, to warn us of its dangers. From years of indulgence, he comes to a very modern conclusion: "Don't go there, girlfriend!" Often, students perceive God as the cosmic killjoy, forbidding all of life's pleasures and requiring that life be confined to a monastery. Impress upon them that this is far from the truth. God created all pleasure in the world. All Satan can do is convince us to misuse it—either in excess or outside of the proper context. God created all pleasure and it is good—we've just been convinced to ruin his gifts by becoming slaves to the world's abuse of it.

This session should open your students' eyes to the emptiness and dissatisfaction that come from pursuing worldly pleasures. True enjoyment comes from contentment that God is in control.

> **LESSON TEXT**
> Ecclesiastes 2:1-11, 17-26
>
> **LESSON FOCUS**
> True enjoyment comes from God.
>
> **LESSON GOALS**
> As a result of participating in this session, students will:
> - See pursuit of the world and indulging their desires as empty.
> - Learn to find satisfaction in today.
> - Discover that purpose in life cannot be found apart from God.

SIGHTING THE STORM

1 Too Much Is Enough

Ask for five volunteers to come to the front of your meeting room. Give each one a 3" x 5" card with a description written on it. You may use the following list or pick your own: weight lifting, eating, suntanning, Internet surfing and dieting. Tell your volunteers that they must pantomime a person who performs this activity to its unhealthy extreme, someone who engages in this activity 24/7. What would they look like? Let them go into another room for a few minutes to give each other ideas and to work on their performances.

While they are outside the room, say to the other students: **"These brave volunteers are going to return one by one to put on a little show for you. They are going to act out a person who has had too much of a good thing, someone who spends too much time**

Materials needed:
3" x 5" cards

Check This...

Show the "Hammered" segment from *Shock Wave, Vol. 2*. A teen explains his various vices and how indulging them does not harm him, even though he repeatedly hits himself with a hammer.

Check This . . .

Play Switchfoot's song "New Way to Be Human," from their *New Way to Be Human* release.

Materials needed:
Blank paper; writing utensils; Bible

Check This . . .

Play the scene from *Indiana Jones and the Last Crusade* that begins at 12:30 and lasts 1 1/2 minutes. It depicts Indy's ship sinking at the beginning of the film. (You could show any shipwreck from any movie.)

Check This . . .

Play the theme to "Gilligan's Island" from *Television's Greatest Hits: '50s & '60s* while your students work in their groups.

Materials needed:
Bibles; reproducible student sheet on page 22 of this book; writing utensils

---

on one activity. Your job will be to guess that activity."

Ask your volunteers to come in one by one and give their performances. Let students shout out their guesses. If a performer is not presenting a clear picture, give enough hints for the group to guess the correct answer. Once all five students have performed, thank them for their awesome pantomimes. Then ask students to break into groups of five. Let them discuss these questions in groups:
- **Are the overdone activities you just saw wrong?**
- **What makes them bad for you?**
- **Why do we take too much of a good thing and make it harmful?**
- **At what point does something become too much?**
- **Do you have too much of anything in your life?**
- **If yes, what can you do to regain balance?**

2 Gilligan's Isle

Distribute blank paper and writing utensils to each student. Ask your students to form groups of four, possibly by favorite vacation destination—the beach, mountains, theme park, etc. Share the following scenario:

"**Each of you has been stranded on an uninhabited desert island. Lucky for you, one crate from your ship also landed on shore. This crate contains five items. You can choose whatever single items you want. These will be the only things you will have on the island with you. In addition to your five items, you can select a lifetime supply of one food item and one drink.**"

Let your students list their choices and share them with their group. Then have them discuss the following:
- **Why did you choose the items you did?**
- **How long would it take you to get bored with your stuff and sick of your food and drink?**
- **Is there anything you used to love but eventually got sick of? If so, why?**

Read Ecclesiastes 2:1-11 aloud to the group. Ask:
- **What did Solomon think of all of his stuff?**
- **Is there anything that promises to always satisfy and never leave you bored?**

ENTERING THE EYE

1 Smells Like a Lost Spirit

Ask everyone to break into groups of three. Then ask students to discuss these questions in their groups:
- **When were you the most depressed in life?**
- **What gave you hope to continue through such a tough time?**

Have students take turns reading Ecclesiastes 2:1-11, 17-26 aloud to each other. When they finish, ask:
- **Would these verses offer much hope without God?**

18   Lesson 2

- What point is there to life without God?

Comment, "A famous man was in the same position as Solomon. He had fame, fortune, popularity, talent—anything he wanted was within his reach. At the pinnacle, he looked out over everything under the sun and realized it was all worthless. Unfortunately, he never lifted his eyes above the sun, so he came to the conclusion that life wasn't worth living since it was empty. That man was Kurt Cobain."

Distribute the reproducible student sheet located on page 22 of this book. Allow students plenty of time to read it over and discuss in their groups. Once they finish, ask for a few volunteers to stand and read what they would have said to Mr. Cobain in his time of need. Then, conclude this activity by asking:

- Do any of you know anyone in despair like Kurt Cobain was?
- What can you do to help them?
- Where will you look for help in times of despair?

2 Fashion Victims

Take volunteers (as many as you have outfits for) and pull them into a side room. Provide each of them with an outfit to wear. These outfits should vary by era of fashion—the '50s, '60s, '70s, '80s and '90s, and any other styles you choose. Make sure each outfit is obviously out of style. Explain to them that they will put on a fashion show for the other students. Tell them where the runway is in the meeting room and instruct them to come out immediately after the person in front of them finishes his or her run. Remind them to ham up their "runway strut" as much as possible. While they pull their outfits on, go back to the main room and explain to the remaining students:

"You are about to witness a very special fashion show. The fashions you will see were the hottest things—decades ago. Your job is to cheer on the runway models and try to guess what era their fashions are from. Let's see the first model!"

After each model has shown his or her "stuff" and the era of clothing has been guessed by the audience, ask the group:

- What are some clothes that were fashionable two years ago that you do not wear anymore?
- What is the hot fad right now? Do you think this trend will last?

Ask your students to break up into groups of five and have them takes turns reading Ecclesiastes 2:1-11 aloud to each other. Then, let them discuss these questions:

- Are any of the things Solomon "studied" in fashion now?
- What will be the result of these fads?
- Does knowing the end result keep you from trying it? Why or why not?
- Which is the most attractive "fad" in Solomon's list in vv. 1-11?
- Why does it appeal so much to you?
- Is that activity a complete waste of time?
- What makes the activity meaningless?

Check This . . .

Play Third Day's song "My Hope Is You," from their *Conspiracy No. 5* album.

Check This . . .

Read the lyrics from Creed's song "What's This Life For?", from their *My Own Prison* album. The singer answers his friend's suicide note by telling him to seek God. (CAUTION: Do not play the song because it includes the profanity from the original suicide letter.)

Materials needed:
Several outfits; Bibles

Check This . . .

Play Jill Sobule's song, "Supermodel," from the *Clueless* soundtrack or "Superstar," by All Star United, from their *International Anthems for the Human Race* album while the runway models perform.

Check This . . .

Have a few Polaroid® cameras or hand out several disposable cameras for students to take pictures of the models as they walk down the runway. Develop the film and have it ready for display next week.

Materials needed:
TV; VCR; Bibles; reproducible student sheet on page 23 of this book

LIVING TO TELL

1. Bored to Tears

Hand out the reproducible student sheet located on page 23 of this book. After giving students a few minutes of tedium, ask:
- **How many of you are bored?**
- **How many of you enjoy busy work?**

Introduce the video by asking, "**Do any of you relate to this movie clip?**"

Show the clip from the movie *Ferris Bueller's Day Off* that begins at 10:45 into the film and lasts a little longer than one minute. This classic clip presents the extreme boredom of a class during an economics lecture.

Once the video clip is over and the laughter dies down, ask your students to form groups of six and take turns telling about the time they were the most bored in their lives. (Hopefully, none of the stories will involve the church!)

Once everyone shares, have each group pick the best story out of its six. Allow the person with the best story from each group to come to the front and share his boredom woes with the entire group. After all the stories have been told, ask:
- **Do you ever relate boredom to God?**
- **Does God want us to be bored?**

In their groups of six, have students take turns reading Ecclesiastes 2:17-26 aloud. Then ask:
- **According to verse 24, what brings happiness? Do you agree with this?**
- **What are some things you do to break the monotony of life?**

2. Building a Better Tomorrow

Materials needed:
Building blocks or Legos®; Bibles; reproducible student sheet on page 24 of this book

Have enough blocks or Legos® so that every student has one piece. Pass them out to each student. Depending on the size of your group, you may want to divide students into more than one "sculpture." Once everyone has a block, explain the activity.

"**We are going to work together to make some art. Each of you will take turns adding your block to the building. The catch is, you must all remain silent. No one can talk or make hand motions or anything that would direct someone else concerning where to put the block. Each of you must add your block and then walk away, letting the people behind you finish it. Line up in alphabetical order according to your last names and start on your masterpiece.**"

Let each student add his piece to the work of art. When it is completed, lift the ban on talking and let students admire their joint creation. Then ask:
- **What do you think of your "sculpture"?**
- **Did it turn out like you thought it would?**

Lesson 2

- **Who had a hard time not telling other people what to do?**
- **Why did you have such a struggle?**

Reread Ecclesiastes 2:18-21, this time from *The Message*:

"And I hated everything I'd accomplished and accumulated on this earth. I can't take it with me—no, I have to leave it to whoever comes after me. Whether they're worthy or worthless—and who's to tell?—they'll take over the earthly results of my intense thinking and hard work. Smoke. That's when I called it quits, gave up on anything that could be hoped for on this earth. What's the point of working your fingers to the bone if you hand over what you worked for to someone who never lifted a finger for it?" Then ask:

- **Why is leaving your work to someone else meaningless?**
- **Have you experienced similar problems when doing a group project at school?**
- **What is Solomon's response to this dilemma? (See vv. 24-26.)**
- **How can you apply this knowledge to your life today?**

Distribute the midweek devotional, **Calculating the Data,** and encourage students to complete the activity this week.

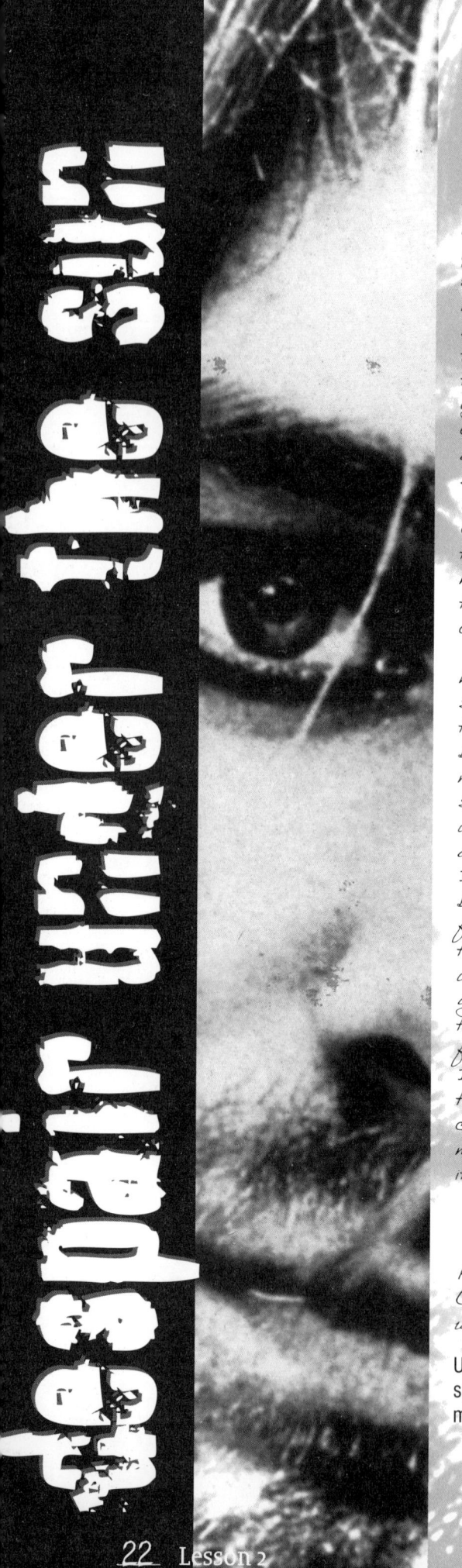

despair under the sun

Speaking from the tongue of an experienced simpleton who obviously would rather be an emasculated, infantile complainer. This note should be pretty easy to understand. All the warnings from the Punk Rock 101 Courses over the years, it's my first introduction to the, shall we say, ethics involved with independence and the embracement of your community has been proven to be very true. I haven't felt the excitement of listening to, as well as creating music, along with really writing something for too many years now. I feel guilty beyond words about these things, for example when we're backstage and the lights go out and the manic roar of the crowd begins. It doesn't affect me in the way which it did for Freddie Mercury, who seemed to love and relish the love and admiration from the crowd, which is something I totally admire and envy. The fact is, I can't fool you, any of you. It simply isn't fair to you, or to me. The worst crime I can think of would be to pull people off by faking it, pretending as if I'm having 100% fun. Sometimes I feel as though I should have a punch-in time clock before I walk out onstage. I've tried everything within my power to appreciate it, and I do, God believe me, I do, but it's not enough. I appreciate the fact that I, and we, have affected, and entertained a lot of people. I must be one of the narcissists who only appreciate things when they're alone. I'm too sensitive, I need to be slightly numb in order to regain the enthusiasm.

But, what's sad is our child. On our last three tours, I've had a much better appreciation of all the people I've known personally, and as fans of our music. But I still can't get out the frustration, the guilt, and the sympathy I have for everybody. There is good in all of us, and I simply love people too much. So much that it makes me feel too sad. The sad little sensitive unappreciative Pisces! Why don't you just enjoy it? I don't know! I have a goddess of a wife who sweats ambition and empathy, and a daughter who reminds me too much of what I used to be. Full of love and joy, every person she meets because everyone is good and will do her no harm. And that terrifies me to the point where I can barely function. I can't stand the thought of Frances becoming the miserable self-destructive, deathrocker I've become. I have it good, very good, and I'm grateful, but since the age of seven, I've become hateful towards all humans in general. Only because it seems so easy for people to get along and have empathy. Empathy only because I love and feel for people too much I guess. Thank you from the pit of my burning nauseous stomach for your letters and concern during the last years. I'm too much of a neurotic moody person and I don't have the passion anymore, so remember, it's better to burn out, than fade away.

Peace, love, empathy,
Kurt Cobain

Frances and Courtney, I'll be at your altar. Please keep going, Courtney, for Frances, for her life which will be so much happier without me. I LOVE YOU. I LOVE YOU!

Underline any portions of the note that echo Solomon's writings in Ecclesiastes. Then, in the space below, write your response to Kurt if you had been able to talk with him before he made his tragic final decision.

22 Lesson 2

©2000 by Standard Publishing. Permission is granted to reproduce this page for ministry purposes only—not for resale.

Calculating The Data

Every mother says it: "Sometimes you just have to do things you don't want to do." That annoying line has been handed down from generation to generation ever since Eve made Abel clean his room. On the other hand, there are some things you never get tired of doing. In the space below, list your three most hated duties in the world. Then, list the three things you most love to do.

Most hated

1.

2.

3.

Most loved

1.

2.

3.

- Why do you hate the "duties" so much?

- What makes the things you love enjoyable?

- Read Ecclesiastes 2:24 and write it in your own words.

- How can you apply this advice to your hated duties to make them more enjoyable?

Circle the hated duty above that you want to enjoy. Pray that God would change your heart and open your eyes. Repeat this prayer every time you must suffer through your task and see if it becomes more enjoyable during this week.

3 Chasing Moments

These are two of history's favorite parental catch phrases: "There's a time and a place for that behavior" and "Life isn't fair." The majority of teens longingly wait for more concrete answers to their queries as to why these statements are true. Solomon asks these same questions in Ecclesiastes and with his God-given wisdom comes up with a better answer than the typical "because I said so."

First, Solomon writes some of the world's best-known Scripture with his list of everything in life. He categorizes every action under the sun and simply states there is a time and a place for every action. The '60s band, The Byrds, recorded his thoughts on their song "Turn, Turn, Turn." Students just need to follow the Holy Spirit's guidance concerning the proper times.

Second, Solomon observes that bad things happen to good people and vice versa. He encourages us to take pleasure in the simple things in life, for this is all we can do. This is the best free advice on the market. Encourage your students to take it. Solomon also affirms God's perfection. Even though we do not always understand, his ways are above scrutiny and reproach. Finally, Solomon applauds a good, faithful friend, pointing out how two people stand strong against trial and temptation while one is overwhelmed.

This session should help your students see that a loving God is behind all the madness out there, that the emotions he has placed in them have proper times of expression and that a Christian friend to whom they can be accountable is priceless.

LESSON TEXT
Ecclesiastes 3:1-14; 4:1-12

LESSON FOCUS
Every godly action has a purpose.

LESSON GOALS
As a result of participating in this session, students will:
- Learn that every action has a proper time.
- See God's work as perfect.
- Desire meaningful, lifelong relationships with other Christians.

Sighting the Storm

1. Time to Spend, Time to Burn

Distribute writing utensils and a copy of the student sheet on page 30 to every student. Allow sufficient time for students to read the information on the sheet.

Walk around the room as they complete the Scripture study and help them if they need it. Then, read Ecclesiastes 3:1-11 aloud, asking students to take turns reading a verse.

After you have finished reading the Scripture, ask, **"Have you ever said, 'I wish I had more time to do this or that'?"** (Allow students to respond.)

Continue by saying, **"Often time seems to fly by at an incredible**

Materials needed:
Bibles; reproducible student sheet on page 30 of this book; writing utensils

Check This . . .
Surprise! Play The Byrds' song "Turn, Turn, Turn," from their *20 Greatest Hits*.

25

pace. Other times it limps along, especially if we can't wait for some big event. Time waits for no one. Yesterday is history. Tomorrow is a mystery. Today is a gift. That's why it's called the present. God has provided all the time we need to accomplish what's really important. Unfortunately, sometimes we don't use wisely the time he gives us. The clock is running. God is concerned about how we make the most of today. Let's see what else Solomon has to say about the subject."

2 How's That Leather Taste?

Depending on the size of your group (either everyone can share or you can ask for several volunteers), take the beginning of your meeting to share embarrassing moments. These should not be just any moment, but a time when a student shoved his foot in his mouth by saying or doing something at the absolute worst time. For example, someone may have asked a girl how her boyfriend was minutes after she was dumped by him, or someone may have asked a person how work was going after he just got fired. After everyone shares, ask students to form groups of four to answer the following questions:

- **What do you want to do when you stick your foot in your mouth?**
- **Why is it so embarrassing?**
- **How can you avoid making a similar mistake again?**
- **Would what you did be acceptable if it had been at a different time?**
- **Why does timing play such an important part in how our words and actions are received?**

Then, ask groups to read Ecclesiastes 3:1-8 to see that there is a time and place for everything.

ENTERING THE EYE

1 Your Tone of Voice Says...

Recruit five students to participate in a short drama. One person will deliver the following line repeatedly to the other four actors: "Cletus, the barn burned down with the cow inside!" The four remaining actors must all deliver the same line: "We're ruined! We'll have to sell everything we own!" Each person delivering this line will be given the emotion they should use when delivering it. The different emotions you will mention to the four students are happy, angry, bored and devastated. If possible, have some funny farming props or costumes like overalls, pitchforks and fake farm animals for the actors to use. After each thespian gives his interpretation of the line, say: **"Obviously, some of these reactions were off base. It's not a time to be happy when tragedy strikes. God gave us a wide range of emotions; he made life full of peaks and valleys, and there are**

Materials needed:
Bibles

Check This...

Play Toad the Wet Sprocket's song "Stupid," from their album *Dulcinea*.

Materials needed:
Bibles; props and costumes

proper times for all of these emotions."

Ask for a volunteer to read aloud Ecclesiastes 3:1-8, if you haven't already done so. Then discuss these questions:

- **Do any of these "times" strike you as wrong all the time? Why?**
- **What circumstances or attitudes can make them all right?**
- **Why does God allow times for things like mourning and war?**
- **When would be a time to hate?**
- **Have you ever been in this situation?**

Reread Ecclesiastes 3:2, this time from *The Message:* "A right time to plant and another to reap." Remind students that even though they probably are not farmers or gardeners, this verse still applies to them. Ask:

- **How do you plant in your personal life?**
- **What types of things should you "plant" in your life?**
- **Are you taking the time to plant these things?**
- **Is there anything in your life right now that you should "uproot"?**

2. Lucky Stars

Before the session, cut out several small pieces of paper, enough for everyone to get a piece. Put a star on one out of every seven pieces. (If your group is smaller than twenty, you may want to put a star on every fourth paper or so.) Mix up the papers and place them in a bowl.

To begin this activity, pass around the bowl to your students and have them pick out one piece of paper and pass it on. Once everyone has a paper, give these instructions: **"Everyone who has a star on his paper should come to the front of the room with me. Everyone else needs to go to the back right-hand corner of the room."**

Once everyone has moved to the proper place (check to make sure the people with stars really have them), bring out the plates of snacks. Bring a steaming hot pizza for them to eat to the front of the room, where you should have only a few students with plenty of room to lounge. Make sure that the person who brings it out walks directly past the mass of students in the corner.

When the students in the front are happily munching on their pizza, bring out a bowl of popcorn for the other students in the back. Hand out one popped kernel of corn to each student. Let them watch their "rich" friends feast for a while before letting the "poor" students return to their seats. Then, discuss these questions:

- **Was the way we divided up the food fair?**
- **How did the popcorn people feel about watching others eat pizza?**
- **How did the pizza people feel eating in front everyone?**

Comment, **"You just took part in a very basic poverty simulation. We quickly broke the group into a percentage that mirrors**

Materials needed:
Pieces of paper; star stickers or a marker; bowl; pizza; popcorn; Bibles

Check This . . .

Play Sherri Youngward's song "Broadway," from her *Faces, Memories, Places* album.

the world's population of the poor and the wealthy." (If you did not use the 1 in 10 ratio because of your group size, point out the correct percentage.) **"In case you were wondering, *everyone* in the United States is considered wealthy since we have an abundance of food and material goods. Most countries struggle to feed everyone daily."**

Read Ecclesiastes 4:1-12 aloud together. Then have students discuss these questions:

- **Why doesn't God start everyone out the same?**
- **Do you deserve all the blessings you have received?**
- **Do you ever wonder why you were born here and not somewhere else in the world?**
- **How can we help people who have much less?**

LIVING TO TELL

1 Safety in Numbers

Ask your students to form groups of four. Instruct the oldest person in each group to stand apart from the group and claim a piece of ground in the room. The remaining three people should try to push the person off balance (not hard), making him move his feet. Let everyone take turns being the single person. Then, have students discuss these questions in their groups:

- **What was it like being the lone person trying to stand strong?**
- **Do you ever feel like this at school? at home? in the world?**

Ask the oldest and the youngest people in each group to join arms and try to stand their ground while the other two people attempt to force them off their spot. After a minute, have the duos change spots.

Finally, ask the three oldest people to link arms and stand their ground against the youngest person, who can try and move them off their spot. After a minute, bring the group back together and ask them to read Ecclesiastes 4:9-12 aloud. Then, they can discuss these questions:

- **Was it difficult to get the trios to move?**
- **How did it feel being alone and trying to move the other three people?**
- **What does Solomon say we should do?**
- **Do you have support like this in your life?**
- **Would you stand firm against temptation if you did?**
- **What is the strongest "cord" you can have in your life?**
- **What are some things you can do to strengthen Jesus' cord in your life?**

Materials needed:
Bibles

Check This . . .
Play dc Talk's song "Lean on Me," from their *Free at Last* album or "Let's Stand Together," recorded by The Kry on their release *I'll Find You There*.

Check This . . .
Show the clip from *The Muppet Movie* that begins at 1:19:30 and runs for 3 minutes. In the scene, Kermit faces off against Doc Hopper and his goons alone, only to prevail when his friends stand strong with him.

28   Lesson 3

2 In Search of...

Before the meeting, hide a 100 Grand® candy bar somewhere in the room, preferably someplace that would take a while to find. Begin this activity by saying, **"Somewhere in this room I have hidden 100 grand. If anyone gets hurt or anything gets damaged, you forfeit the prize. Otherwise, the first person to find it gets to keep it."**

Allow everyone to search the room (with your damage control supervision). After someone discovers the candy and the room calms down, break into groups of three and distribute copies of the reproducible student sheet found on page 31. Before having them complete the sheets, ask students:

- **How long would you have searched for the 100 grand?**
- **What's the hardest you have ever searched for something?**
- **Have you ever given up searching for something that was really important to you? Why or why not?**

Ask them to read Ecclesiastes 3:9-14 aloud in their groups. Then let them discuss these questions:

- **What does it mean that God has "set eternity in the hearts of men"?**
- **Did you search for God? How long?**
- **How did you finally "find" Christ?**

Ask students to complete their sheets in their groups. Then, encourage them to close by praying for each other—that they will clearly see the path to Christ and for boldness in pointing others to the path.

Distribute the midweek devotional, **Calculating the Data,** and encourage students to complete the activity this week.

Materials needed:
Bibles; reproducible student sheets on pages 31, 32 of this book; writing utensils; 100 Grand® bar

Check This...

Play the U2 song "Still Haven't Found What I'm Looking For," from their album *The Joshua Tree* while the students search for the 100 Grand® bar.

Time to Spend, Time to Burn

Imagine there is a bank account that credits your account each morning with $86,400. It carries over no balance from day to day. Every evening the bank deletes whatever part of the balance you failed to use during the day. What would you do? Draw out every cent, of course!

Each of us has a bank. Its name is TIME. Every morning, it credits you with 86,400 seconds. Every night it writes off, as lost, whatever of this you have failed to invest to a good purpose. It carries over no balance. Each day it opens a new account for you. Each night it burns the remains of the day. If you fail to use the day's deposits, the loss is yours. There is no going back. You must live in the present on today's deposits.

To realize the value of ONE YEAR, ask a student who failed a grade in school.

To realize the value of ONE MONTH, ask a mother who gave birth to a premature baby.

To realize the value of ONE WEEK, ask the editor of a weekly newspaper.

To realize the value of ONE DAY, ask a postal delivery person.

To realize the value of ONE HOUR, ask two people in love who are waiting to meet.

To realize the value of ONE MINUTE, ask a person who missed a plane.

To realize the value of ONE SECOND, ask a person who just avoided an accident.

To realize the value of ONE MILLISECOND, ask the person who won a silver medal in the Olympics.

What do the following Scripture verses say about our use of time?

- **Job 14:5, 6**

- **Psalm 31:14, 15**

- **Ephesians 5:15, 16**

Lesson 3

In Search of...

Everyone is looking for God; people just don't know it. God placed a hole in our hearts that only he can fill, but people usually try to fill it with other things.

Write on the forehead of the person at the right the name of someone you know who is searching. Fill in the other shapes with the different things this person is trying to fill his or her God-sized hole with.

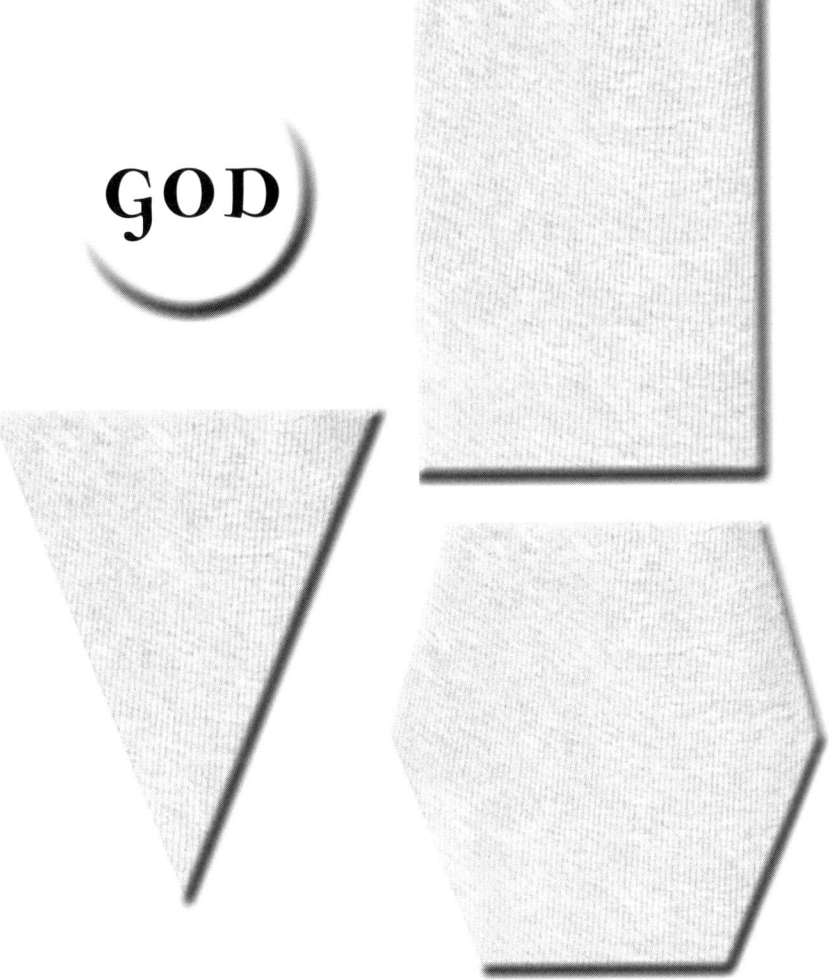

GOD

What are some ways you can point your friend to God?

©2000 by Standard Publishing. Permission is granted to reproduce this page for ministry purposes only—not for resale.

31

Calculating The Data

You've read the verses and sung the song a million times. Now it's time to put it in your own words for easy application to your life. Fill in the blanks below with your own words and phrases to personalize the passage and bring it into the new millennium. Look at the original lines in Ecclesiastes 3:1-8 for help.

There is a time for everything,

and a _____ for every activity _____:

a time to _____ and a time to _____

a time to _____ and a time to _____

a time to _____ and a time to _____

a time to _____ and a time to _____

a time to _____ and a time to _____

a time to _____ and a time to _____

a time to _____ and a time to _____

a time to _____ and a time to _____

a time to _____ and a time to _____

a time to _____ and a time to _____

a time to _____ and a time to _____

a time to _____ and a time to _____

a time to _____ and a time to _____

a time to _____ and a time to _____.

4 CHASING SATISFACTION

Parents often complain about teens not showing the respect due their elders. Kids disregard and disrespect their words and actions to their face, claiming independence earlier than expected or deserved. The parents grumble, but do not take responsibility for the trouble they brought on themselves.

Solomon speaks right into this twenty-first century from his tenth century B.C. palace living room, exposing all the roots of this problem within the fifth chapter of his journal under the sun. First, he berates our lackadaisical and flippant approach to God. In our day, it is commonplace for promises to people to be broken. A promise to God lies even lower on the totem pole than those to human beings. Students learn to enter God's throne room, wheel and deal for their desires, and leave again without even a tip of the hat.

Next, Solomon berates the great American beast—wealth. He points out the hollow pursuit of the American Dream, the elusive ideal our elders have preached and pursued for decades. Solomon then explains the remedy for this national disease—contentment with God's blessings. These verses hold a radically different worldview than the one we now hold. Hopefully, your students will grab onto the wise words that have been scoffed at for years.

This session will give your students a new appreciation for the holiness and majesty of God, help them put money and material possessions in their proper place and find contentment with where they are and what they have.

> **LESSON TEXT**
> Ecclesiastes 5
>
> **LESSON FOCUS**
> Instead of being greedy, we should seek to be content with God's provisions.
>
> **LESSON GOALS**
> As a result of participating in this session, students will:
> - Understand that God is to be honored and revered.
> - See that wealth and money will never satisfy desire.
> - Choose their words wisely, since they are accountable for them.
> - Find contentment in their life.

SIGHTING THE STORM

1. King (or Queen) for an Evening

Before the meeting, tape a 3" x 5" card which reads "You are anointed" underneath one of the chairs. Once all your students are seated, announce: **"One of you is about to become royalty for the evening! Look under your chair to see if you have a 3" x 5" card anointing you king or queen. If you do, bring it up here to receive your crown."**

Let students check their seats. When the winner finds the card and comes up to the front of the room, have him or her sit in the "throne." Crown the newly anointed and hand him or her the scepter. Play some royal "coronation" music to make it even more eventful. If no one sits

Materials needed:
Throne; crown; scepter; Bibles; 3" x 5" card; CD player; coronation music

33

Check This . . .
Play Five Iron Frenzy's song "Banner Year," from their *Our Newest Album Ever!* album.

Check This . . .
Perform the skit "Now Presenting," from *Sanctified Skits, Vol. 1*. This sketch shows several different people approaching a king and the different (incorrect) ways they treat a man due great respect (like we often treat God in prayer).

Materials needed:
Scratch paper; writing utensils; paper shredder; Bibles

Check This . . .
Play a clip from the movie *Hope Floats* that begins at 1:42:15 and lasts for two minutes. This heart-wrenching scene shows a father breaking a promise to his young daughter that she can live with him. The daughter completely breaks down as he drives away, shattering his promise and her dreams.

Materials needed:
Game-show preparations; dollar bills; game board; blank paper; writing utensils; Bibles

---

in the correct seat, crown the person who sat closest to the card.

Comment, "**(Student's name) is king (or queen) for the evening. I would like everyone to line up and pay homage to our leader.**" Give the students an opportunity to approach the "royal person" and pay homage in their own way. Ask them to sit down once everyone has had a chance (while the winner remains seated on the throne). Then, discuss these questions:

- **What was it like approaching royalty?**
- **Would you respect (student's name) as your king (or queen)?**

Read Ecclesiastes 5:1-7 aloud to the group. Then ask:

- **Do you respect God as the ruler of your life? Why or why not?**
- **How do you typically treat him when you approach his throne?**
- **Is that how you would approach him if he were sitting on a throne before you like (student's name) is?**
- **How can you change your attitude toward approaching God?**

After discussing these questions, the royal person may return to the rest of the group.

2 Broken Promises

As students enter the room, ask them to take a piece of scratch paper and something to write with. After all students have arrived, give them these instructions: "**Take a minute to write down a promise you have recently broken. It can be a promise you made to a friend, family member, God, a teacher or yourself. Be honest. No one else will see what you have written.**"

Once everyone finishes writing down the broken promise, ask students to line up and one by one put their promises through the paper shredder. (Use a paper cutter if you don't have a paper shredder.) When everyone has done so, ask these questions:

- **How did it feel to shred your promise?**
- **How do you think the person to whom you broke your promise felt about your failure to keep your word?**

Ask everyone to read Ecclesiastes 5:1-7 silently to themselves. Then ask:

- **Do you ever break promises to God?**
- **Why is this foolish?**
- **Does God expect us to make any promises to him?**
- **Why do you do it?**
- **What was the last promise you made to God?**
- **Did you keep it?**
- **What would help you take your promises to God more seriously?**

ENTERING THE EYE

Money Hungry

This activity will take a little more preparation, but should really drive home the point. As best you can, before the meeting

34 Lesson 4

turn your room into the set of a game show. You will need places for three contestants to stand and a podium for you to stand behind as game-show host. Create a "question board" that everyone in the room will be able to see. (Try to use PowerPoint® for your questions and answers. If this is not an option, use either a chalkboard or butcher paper.) The board will contain both the questions and the answers, though the answers should not be revealed until after the contestants attempt to correctly guess them.

Take the three students with the birthdays closest to the day of your meeting to be your contestants. Give each contestant several sheets of blank paper and something to write with. The game is simple: if contestants answer the question correctly, they receive $1. Reveal the first of the three questions on the board and allow the contestants 30 seconds to record their answers.

The three questions you ask the contestants should be extremely simple, practically guaranteeing they will get them correct. Here are some examples:
- **Our pastor's name is . . . .**
- **Jesus had how many disciples?**
- **Who is Luke Skywalker's father?**
- **Who is the President of the United States?**
- **The United States has how many states?**
- **John, Paul, George and Ringo made up what famous British band?**

Ask the contestants to show their answers to the studio audience before you reveal the correct answer. (You may wish to choose someone to serve as "Vanna" to reveal the answers if you wish.)

After the contestants answer the three questions, say: **"You now have a choice. You can either sit down now and keep the money you have won or put it on the line by trying to answer the Final Challenge question. If you answer it correctly, you will add $10 to the money you have already won. If you answer incorrectly, you lose any prize money you already have."**

Allow the contestants to make their decision, either to keep the money or go for the big payoff. For those who decide to stay, give them thirty seconds to answer an impossible question such as **"Who succeeded Elah as King of Israel?"** or **"What is the GNP of Zimbabwe?"** (Whatever question you choose, be sure to have the correct answer handy.) After they miss the question and return any of their previous winnings, ask the contestants:
- **Why did you risk your winnings on the challenge question?**
- **Why did you decide to keep your money and not risk it?**

Ask several students to take turns reading Ecclesiastes 5:8-17 aloud to the group. Let the contestants and the rest of the students form groups of four to discuss the following questions:
- **Why do we love money?**
- **Will we ever have enough?**
- **Does verse 10 describe anyone you know?**

Check This . . .
Play the theme song from *Jeopardy* during the game show.

Check This . . .
Show the clip from *Indiana Jones and the Last Crusade* that begins at 1:56:45 and runs for one minute. The scene shows how greed for the Holy Grail brings only harm.

- **Does this person seem happy?**
- **How do your parents view money?**
- **Why does wealth never bring complete satisfaction?**

Ask students to read Matthew 19:16-26, then answer these questions:

- **Do you think it is that hard for a rich man to enter Heaven? Why or why not?**
- **Do these passages change your perspective on money?**
- **What are some practical ways you can ensure that your money never becomes your master?**

2 You Can't Take It with You

Bring a pile of junk from your office, closet and garage and dump it on the floor of your meeting room. Make sure you have more stuff laid out than could possibly fit inside the suitcase you bring with you. Depending on the size of your group, either allow everyone to try this exercise or take a few volunteers. Instruct the packers to somehow get all of the objects into the suitcase. (If you value the suitcase you provide, actively monitor their packing and warn them that anyone who ruins the case will be sent home in it.)

After students have struggled with the dilemma long enough, or simply given up, have them form groups of four and read Ecclesiastes 5:8-17 aloud in their groups. Pass out copies of the student sheet on page 38 for students to complete. Say, "**Contrary to popular belief, you can't take it with you. In fact, you don't even get to take your body with you to Heaven. Your stuff all stays here to rust and rot and be used and fought over by your relatives. Fill out and discuss this sheet in your groups.**" After they have done so, bring the whole group back together. Tape butcher paper on the wall or use a chalkboard to write down students' responses to these questions:

- **What things did you decide we can take to Heaven with us?**
- **As a youth group, are we investing in eternal or temporal possessions?**
- **Which of the things you listed can we pack as a youth group?**

Circle their choices on the butcher paper or chalkboard. Then, continue by asking:

- **What are two concrete ways we as a youth group can pursue these eternal things?**
- **Why do we constantly seek to accumulate material wealth?**
- **How can too much wealth "harm" you? (v. 13).**
- **What are you going to do differently this week in light of this Scripture?**

LIVING TO TELL

1 Your Most Perfect Day

Pass out copies of the reproducible found on page 39 to students and have them complete the activity. Allow five

---

Materials needed:
Suitcase; lots of junk; reproducible student sheet on page 38 of this book; Bibles; writing utensils; butcher paper; marker; masking tape

Check This . . .
Show the clip from *Willy Wonka and the Chocolate Factory* that starts at 1:20:15 and lasts for three minutes. In the clip, Veruca Salt selfishly sings about wanting every material possession and wanting them all now.

Check This . . .
Play Burlap to Cashmere's song "Treasures in Heaven," from their *Anybody Out There?* release while students complete the sheets.

Check This . . .
Play Satellite Soul's song "Love Is All We Own," from their album entitled *Great Big Universe*.

Materials needed:
Reproducible student sheet on page 39 of this book; writing utensils

minutes for this and, if time permits, ask a few students to share what they wrote. Let them form groups of five to discuss these questions:
- **Why isn't every day of your life a perfect day?**
- **Does God promise that our days will be perfect?**

Ask students to read Ecclesiastes 5:18-20 aloud. Or, you might want to read these verses from *The Message*: **"After looking at the way things are on this earth, here's what I've decided is the best way to live: Take care of yourself, have a good time, and make the most of whatever job you have for as long as God gives you life. And that's about it. That's the human lot. Yes, we should make the most of what God gives, both the bounty and the capacity to enjoy it, accepting what's given and delighting in the work. It's God's gift! God deals out joy in the present, the now. It's useless to brood over how long we might live."**

Ask students these questions:
- **What should be our criteria for a perfect day?**
- **What types of things "ruin" your day?**
- **Have you ever had something bad happen, but you didn't let it ruin your day? How did you do that?**
- **What other things can you do to reduce the impact of disappointments?**

Challenge students to memorize Philippians 4:11 this week and recite it to themselves any time their day takes a wrong turn.

2 I Have the Conch

To begin this activity, ask students to form groups of five or six. Bring enough seashells to give one per group. (If you cannot get some seashells, come up with some other object that can serve as the "conch" in each group.) Give groups these instructions: **"Each of you will have exactly one minute to gripe about anything you want. When I say, 'Go,' the first person will pick up the seashell and rant and rave while everyone else must listen without saying a word. When one minute is up, he or she will hand the seashell to the person on the right, who will have one minute to air a beef with the world. We will continue doing this until everyone has had the opportunity to gripe."**

Set the timer, start it and say "Go." When the timer rings, inform everyone to pass the seashell and start again. Once everyone has been allowed to speak, ask students to read Ecclesiastes 5:18-20 aloud to each other, or see the wording in *The Message* in the previous activity. Then, ask students to discuss these questions in their groups:
- **What do these verses mean to you?**
- **Should we spend our time ranting and complaining about our lives? Why or why not?**

Encourage students to think of three things for which they are thankful, then share those with their group. After they finish sharing, have them pray for contentment together, each student naming one attitude God needs to help change.

Distribute the midweek devotional, **Calculating the Data,** and encourage students to complete the activity this week.

Check This . . .

Play The W's song "Alarm Clock," from their *Fourth From the Last* release or the song "Lovely Day," from either Kirk Franklin's *Nu Nation Project* or Out of Eden's *Lovin' the Day* album.

Check This . . .

Show the opening scene of *Pee Wee's Big Adventure* that begins at 1 minute and lasts 1½ minutes. The clip shows Pee Wee's idea of a "dream" day.

Materials needed:
Bibles; seashells; timer; reproducible student sheet on page 40 of this book

You Can't Take It With You

List your 10 favorite possessions below:

1.   6.

2.   7.

3.   8.

4.   9.

5.   10.

- Which of these can you take with you to Heaven?

- What types of things can you take to Heaven?

- Are you currently packing any of these things?

- What can you do this week to start packing your heavenly bag with eternal things?

"Don't hoard treasure down here where it gets eaten by moths and corroded by rust or—worse!—stolen by burglars. Stockpile treasure in heaven, where it's safe from moth and rust and burglars. It's obvious, isn't it? The place where your treasure is, is the place you will most want to be, and end up being" Matthew 6:19-21, *The Message*.

Your Most Perfect Day

Dear Diary,

What an incredible _____ day! I _____
                    (season)   (slept in/got up early)

and _____ breakfast. I went to _____
      (ate/skipped)   (the mall/beach/mountains/movies/friend's house)

to _____. I had a blast hanging with _____. We ate so
     (activity)   (best friend)

much at _____, we nearly barfed. We were ordering some
           (favorite restaurant)

_____ when, no lie, _____ sat with
  (favorite dessert)   (favorite famous person)

us. He/she paid for everything and let us ride around _____ with
                                                         (hometown)

him in his _____. Then we flew to _____
              (favorite car)   (favorite city or foreign country)

to spend the night. What a perfect day!

"I am not saying this because I am in need, for I have learned to be content whatever the circumstances" Philippians 4:11.

139

Calculating The Data

Santa is bankrupt! He didn't know the IRS taxes global gift giving. Because of his folly, there will be no presents this year. Take a look at your returned Christmas list below and see how you'll do during the gift-giving bust.

Dear Santa,
Please send the following:

1.

2.

3.

4.

5.

Next to each present, write something you already have now that you can use in place of this item, or some other way to be content without it.

"Keep your lives free from the love of money and be content with what you have, because God has said, 'Never will I leave you; never will I forsake you'" Hebrews 13:5.

Congratulations! You have survived the gift-giving bust! Pray this week that God will open your eyes to ways you can use or reuse what he has already blessed you with instead of constantly craving more.

5 CHASING ANSWERS

Columbine. That word will stick in your students' memories forever. The horrific tragedy now stands as an icon for all that is wrong in the world—senseless violence, cliques, alienation, unexpected tragedy, injustice, intolerance. The fallout of the massacre has prompted numerous questions about what so many believe and held to be true: Why do bad things happen? How can evil win? Whom do we follow? What could breed so much hatred?

King Solomon continued to observe his surroundings under the sun, even when the world seemed to make no sense. Fortunately, his wisdom provides some much-needed insight into the madness. First, he encourages obedience to life's authorities (which teenagers have plenty of!). Then, Solomon agrees with the teen lament that life isn't fair, but he explains how to overlook this and enjoy life, no matter how crazy it gets. He also takes comfort in the fact that justice, often absent on earth, certainly reigns supreme before the judgment seat of God. Finally, the wisest man in the world states that no man knows everything. Information on every subject known to man awaits our fingertips on the Internet, self-help solutions abound at bookstores and every psychic between Timbuktu and Tucson has a 900 number. It's reassuring to know that they are as clueless as we are about the biggest questions to life. Besides, this gives us plenty to learn when we get to Heaven.

This session should reinforce the need for obedience and trust that God is in perfect control of the earthly chaos and that a Christian can blissfully live in ignorance of worldly concerns.

> **LESSON TEXT**
> Ecclesiastes 8:2-17; 9:11, 12
>
> **LESSON FOCUS**
> Even when things seem bad, we need to trust that God is in control.
>
> **LESSON GOALS**
> As a result of participating in this session, students will:
> - Obey authorities in their lives.
> - Realize that life in the physical world is not fair.
> - Accept that they will not always understand life.

SIGHTING THE STORM

1 Racing the Yellow

Begin this activity by taking your entire group outside. Ask for four volunteers and appoint them as leaders. Once you have chosen them, allow each of them to select an assistant. Have the assistants blindfold their leaders. Gather the group together in the center of the area (grass lot, parking lot, etc.) you choose for this activity. Ask the assistants to direct their leaders to stand outside the group and form a box around them, as if each leader serves as the point on a compass. Once all of the leaders are equidistant from the group and each other, explain the rules of the game:

Materials needed:
Bibles; four blindfolds; chalk and chalkboard

Check This . . .

Play Five Iron Frenzy's song "Faking Life," from their *Upbeats and Downbeats* album.

Check This . . .

Play the secular song "I Fought the Law," by The Clash, from their *The Story of the Clash, Vol. 1* album during the "Red Light, Green Light" game.

Materials needed:
Whiffle ball bat and ball; blindfold; tennis racket; Ping-Pong® paddle; prize; Bibles

Check This . . .

To make the point that life is not fair, show a clip from the *Jesus* film or *Jesus of Nazareth* where Jesus is unfairly tried by his accusers before Pontius Pilate.

"You are going to play 'Red Light, Green Light.' Each of you must choose which leader you are going to run toward. When I say 'Go,' each leader will serve as your stoplight. When they say 'green light,' you can run toward them. When they finish saying 'red light,' you must be completely still. If you are still moving, the assistant will send you back to the start. If you get to the leader, then you will take his place."

If there are no questions, begin the game. Halfway through the game, have the leaders rotate clockwise so that students now have a different leader they must run toward. Anytime a student reaches a leader, let her take the leader's place. Rotate the leaders periodically and play the game until everyone makes it to the leader, or until you get tired.

Once the game is over, take everyone back inside. Then ask, **"How was that game like life?"**

Read Ecclesiastes 8:2-7 aloud to them. Then discuss these questions:

- **How many authorities are in your life right now?** (List students' answers on a chalkboard.)
- **What new authorities do you have coming in your future?**
- **Do all of these people care about your needs?**
- **Why should you follow them?**
- **What will happen if you do?**

Comment, **"In the game we played, your leaders constantly changed. This also happens in life. Your earthly authorities will change. Thankfully, Solomon gives some wise advice for dealing with them. Let's take a deeper look."**

2 All's Fair . . .

Ask for a male and a female volunteer. When you have your two contestants, explain the rules of the game:

"This game is simple. It's similar to baseball. I am going to pitch this whiffle ball to you three times. The person who hits it the most times wins. If there is a tie in the number of times it is hit, the person who hit the ball the farthest wins. The winner will receive (some desirable prize of your choosing). Any questions?"

After answering any questions, let the girl go first. Hand her a tennis racket and take a few steps away from her. Pitch her the whiffle ball and take note of how many times she hits it. Once she is done, turn to the male contestant and say, **"Before you take your turn, we need to make a few adjustments to the game."**

First, take the tennis racket from the young man and hand him a Ping-Pong® paddle. Second, put a blindfold over his eyes so he can't see. Finally, spin him around a few times so he is directionally disoriented. Pitch the whiffle ball three times to the severely challenged male contestant without even telling him when you are pitching. After you pitch three times, congratulate the female contestant and award her the prize. Have both contestants sit down. Then ask students to respond to these questions:

- **Was that game fair? Why not?**
- **Is life fair? Why not?**

Go around the room and take turns reading verses from Ecclesiastes 8:10-17.

Conclude by saying, "Have you ever looked at someone who wasn't honoring God and wondered why they seemed to have it so well? You might be trying to serve God and really having a tough time just getting by. Sometimes life just doesn't seem fair, does it? Let's see what Solomon has to say about how we should deal with this problem."

ENTERING THE EYE

1 The Coronation

Distribute copies of the student sheet found on page 46 of this book. Set out all of the supplies students will need to create their crowns. Allow your students plenty of time to color, cut and glue their crowns together. Once everyone is finished and wearing a crown, ask students to break into groups of three and read Ecclesiastes 8:2-9 aloud. Ask them to think about some of the authorities in their lives such as parents, teachers, coaches and employers. Ask them to think about one of these people in particular and answer the following questions concerning that person:

- **Why is this person the king in your life?**
- **Do you obey this person? Why or why not?**
- **Is he (or she) always fair?** (If the answer is "no," have them share an example of injustice with the group.)
- **Should this affect your obedience?**
- **Why do you think God placed this person in your life?**

Encourage groups to take a few minutes to pray for the authorities in their lives.

Materials needed:
Bibles; markers; crayons; scissors; glue; reproducible student sheet on page 46 of this book; writing utensils

2 The Good, the Bad and the Incomprehensible

Show the clip from the movie *Patch Adams* that begins at 1:32:15 and lasts for two minutes and thirty seconds. In this scene, Robin Williams rages against God, questioning how he could let bad things happen to good people in the wake of his friend's murder. God answers him in the form of a butterfly, showing in a small, quiet way that God is good. After students have viewed the movie clip, discuss these questions:

- **What was Robin Williams asking?**
- **How did God answer him in that butterfly?**
- **Do you ever question God?**
- **Has he ever answered in a tangible way?**

Allow students who so desire to share with the group. When they finish, read Matthew 15:19 aloud to the group. Then ask:

Materials needed:
Bibles; TV; VCR; videotape

- **What does this verse mean?**
- **What is the true source of evil in the world?**

Have everyone form groups of three. Ask the youngest student in each group to read Ecclesiastes 8:14-17 aloud. Then, let them discuss these questions:

- **Does life ever look this way to you?**
- **Why do bad things happen to good people?**
- **Why do people blame God for tragedies?**
- **Will we ever fully understand?**
- **What is Solomon's advice in dealing with this fact?**

LIVING TO TELL

1. O Death, When Is Thy Sting?

Have students form groups of three. Then, give them these instructions: **"Take turns telling each other the date of your birth and any other information about that day you might know—like the name of the hospital, your weight and length, time of day or funny stories your parents have told you."**

After students have all had a chance to share with each other their birth details, ask, **"Can any of you give any of the details surrounding your death? If anyone can, we'd sure like to hear them!"** Pause for a moment. Then read Ecclesiastes 9:11, 12 aloud to the group. Ask students:

- **What do these verses mean to you?**
- **What does verse 12 say about death?**
- **Would you live differently if you knew the exact day of your death like you do the day of your birth?**
- **If yes, what exactly would you do differently?**
- **What keeps you from doing that now?**

Challenge students to live to tell others about Jesus, as if each day were their last day on earth.

2. I Knew That!

Pass out writing utensils and the reproducible student sheet on page 47 and allow your students five minutes to answer the questions. After a few minutes of head scratching, give them the answers:

1. *Anwar Sadat and Menachem Begin*
2. *It Happened One Night*
3. *Thriller*
4. *Dallas Stars*
5. *Near Queensland, Australia*
6. *Your state's flower*
7. *Bill Richards*
8. *Sugar, corn syrup, adipic acid, hydrogenated and palm kernel oils, soybean oil*
9. *Belteshazzar, which means "Bel protect his life"*

Materials needed:
Bibles

Check This . . .
Show a clip from any film with an unexpected death in it. Examples run from the serious (*What Dreams May Come*, *City of Angels* and *Hope Floats*), to the humorous (*The Princess Bride* and *Groundhog Day*). Choose the tone that best fits your group's interests and needs.

Check This . . .
Play Five Iron Frenzy's song "Second Season," from their *Our Newest Album Ever!* release.

Materials needed:
Reproducible student sheets on pages 47, 48 of this book; writing utensils; Bibles

10. Hank Azaria

Comment, **"We live in the information age. We can find the most minute detail on the most obscure subject in seconds. Entire businesses exist simply to move information from one place to another. Even with this information explosion, though, no one knows everything."**

Ask a student to read Ecclesiastes 8:17 aloud to the group. Ask, **"What does this verse mean?"** Allow a few students to answer. Then, discuss these questions:

- **Why do we insist on knowing everything?**
- **Why does God leave so much unanswered?**
- **Do questions strengthen or weaken your faith? Why?**

Close this session by asking students to take a few minutes to pray for God's peace concerning their unanswered questions and increased faith to trust God in these areas. Distribute the midweek devotional, **Calculating the Data,** and encourage students to complete the newspaper activity this week.

Check This . . .

Show the clip from *Groundhog Day* that begins at 1:09:30 and lasts almost three minutes. In the scene, Bill Murray demonstrates to Andie MacDowell that he knows everything about every person in the diner.

The Coronation

Even though we tossed our king out with the tea in the Revolutionary War, every American must obey an honorary monarch. This person could be a parent, a boss, a coach or a teacher. We all fall under someone else's authority at different times in our lives. Draw a crown in the space below. Write the name of your "monarch" on it and then color and decorate it how you wish.

I Knew That!

Answer the questions below:

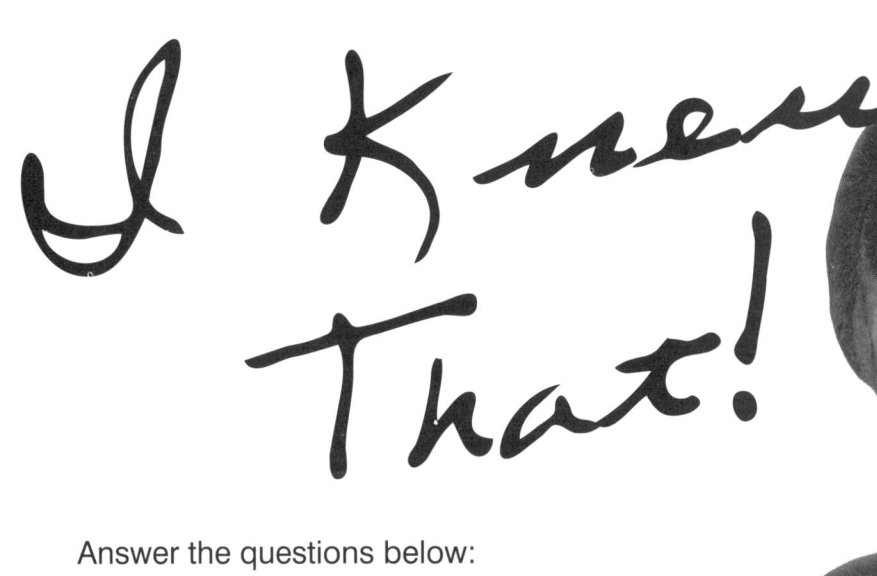

1. Who signed the Camp David Accord?
2. What was the first movie to win Oscars for best picture, director, actor, actress and screenplay?
3. What is the single largest-selling album in history?
4. Who won the Stanley Cup in 1999?
5. Where is the Great Barrier Reef located?
6. What is our state flower?
7. Who invented the skateboard?
8. What are the ingredients for PEZ?
9. What was Daniel's Babylonian name and what does it mean?
10. Who performs the voice of "Apu" on "The Simpsons"?

How did you do?

1-3 correct
You enjoy your hobbies and not much else.

4-7 correct
You know a little something about everything.

8-10 correct
You are a human cyborg with a computer for a brain.

©2000 by Standard Publishing. Permission is granted to reproduce this page for ministry purposes only—not for resale.

Calculating The Data

Read the first section of the most current newspaper you can find. Find a story of injustice in it and paraphrase what happened in the space below.

- What wasn't fair in this situation?

- Can the situation ever be made right again?

- How would you react if you were the victim?

Read Romans 8:28. Does this give you any peace?

Take a few moments to pray for the people involved in the story you read.

6 CHASING GOD

Finally! Like the anticipation for the resolution to a cliffhanger, Solomon, the man granted the most wisdom in history, spills the beans. After trudging through the muck of his life, pulling each dirty piece out for us to examine and discard, he reveals in a mere two verses the meaning of life. Simply stated, the person living a fulfilled, meaningful life spends it serving and obeying God.

That's it? That's the pie in the sky everyone chases? Yup. Submissive obedience is the answer. Now comes the application. O-b-e-y may be easy to spell, but it's difficult to practice all of our days. Just because something is hard, though, does not make it impossible. You need to show your students that it can become reality. By displaying an obedient servant's heart to them in your own life, they will see at least one living example of this fact. Encourage them to set themselves apart from the crowd now, casting aside worldly desires and setting their hearts and eyes on God's kingdom.

This session should reinforce to your students that they should follow God now while they are young. Everything they do, both the good and the bad, the public and the private, will be judged by God.

> **LESSON TEXT**
> Ecclesiastes 11:9–12:14
>
> **LESSON FOCUS**
> Now is the time to pursue God.
>
> **LESSON GOALS**
> As a result of participating in this session, students will:
> - Seek to follow God in their teenage years.
> - Understand that God will judge all of their actions.
> - Commit to keeping God's commands.

SIGHTING THE STORM

1. Outta My Way!

Before the meeting, set up an obstacle course. You can do this either inside or outside, depending on the size of your room and the number of students you have. The course does not have to be elaborate, just enough twists, turns, ducks and jumps to cause even the most athletic person to concentrate. Give everyone a chance to run through the course. Possibly keep time and allow the top three male and female times to run against each other again to win prizes.

After everyone has had an opportunity to run through the course, have them form groups of three and discuss these questions:
- Why is an obstacle course more difficult than a 100-yard dash?
- Which seems more like life, a 100-yard dash or an obstacle course? Why?

Ask students to read Ecclesiastes 11:9–12:14 aloud in their groups. Then ask:
- How does Ecclesiastes 12:1 relate to the obstacle course?
- Why is it important to remember God now?

Materials needed:
Several obstacles; prizes; Bibles

Check This . . .
Show "The Diet" segment from *Shock Wave, Vol. 4*. This parable depicts a man trying to persevere and stay on his diet.

Check This . . .
Play dc Talk's song "What If I Stumble," from their *Jesus Freak* album.

Materials needed:
Bibles

Check This . . .

Show the "Spiritualeyze" segment from *Shock Wave, Vol. 4*. This parable shows vividly the importance of sharing your faith, because every day might be a person's last.

Materials needed:
TV; VCR; videotape; Bibles; writing utensils; reproducible student sheet on page 54 of this book

- Are you doing that?
- What are some of the obstacles in your pursuit of God right now?
- Are you avoiding them or running into them? Why?
- How can you do a better job of avoiding them?

2. Carpe Diem. Servium Christos.

Read the following story to your students:

"Jack pulled the beautiful, handcrafted silk and lace lingerie out of the drawer. He admired it, smiling sadly, and handed it to Judy.

"'What's this?' she asked.

"'Something very special. It's from France. Very delicate, very expensive. It's supposed to be for a very special occasion. I guess we should've made every day a special occasion.'

"Slowly, Jack handed the lingerie to Judy, his sister. She took it. 'It was an accident, Jack. There's no way you could've known.'

"Jack wiped the tears of his wife's death from his eyes. 'Don't wait to do tomorrow what you can do today, Sis. It's not worth it.'" (Author unknown)

After the story has been read, ask students:

- How does that story make you feel?
- Do you treat every day as a special day?
- Is there anything you might be putting off that you should take care of today? Why?

Go around the room and have students take turns reading a verse aloud from Ecclesiastes 11:9–12:14. Then discuss:

- Are you remembering God in your youth like Ecclesiastes 12:1 warns? Why or why not?
- How do Solomon's words agree with the story I just related?

ENTERING THE EYE

1. Skeletons in the Open

Play a clip from the movie *The Truman Show* that begins at 1:01:30 and lasts almost two minutes. The scene explains how Jim Carrey's every move is broadcast 24 hours a day though an elaborate array of cameras. After showing the clip, say, **"It's pretty scary how intrusive technology can be today. It seems like the only place you can go for privacy is your bedroom or camping in the middle of nowhere. Even then, there's probably some spy satellite watching your every move! Really, though, nothing we try to hide remains secret forever. Have any of you ever done something you thought no one, or maybe a certain person or persons, would not see or hear but they did?"**

Allow several students to share their embarrassing stories. Then ask:

- Would you have done or said those things if you thought you

Lesson 6

were going to get caught?

Read Ecclesiastes 12:14 aloud from *The Message*: "**Eventually God will bring everything that we do out into the open and judge it according to its hidden intent, whether it's good or evil.**" Ask students:
- How does that make you feel?
- Are you ever embarrassed by a reminder of God's presence?

Continue by saying, "**Matthew 10:30 says that the very hairs of our head are all numbered. That means that God concerns himself with your welfare and knows everything about you.**"
- How do you think God feels watching you?
- Does he want us to have fun?
- Why does he watch our every move, then?
- How can we possibly be pleasing to God if he watches us all the time?

Distribute writing utensils and copies of the sheet found on page 54 of this book to students and allow them sufficient time to work on the activity. This skeleton evaluation is very personal. Not all students will be able to complete this inner reflection during your session. They may want to take it and finish it at home.

2. Can I See Some ID?

Write the names Joan of Arc, Mozart, Nadia Comaneci, Alexander the Great and Cameron Crowe down the right side of a piece of butcher paper or a chalkboard that everyone in the group can see. Then ask students, "**What did each of these people accomplish in their lives?**"

Record the answers your students call out beside the corresponding name. (Feel free to change any of the names given here for some different young achievers.) Some possible answers for each person are as follows:

Joan of Arc:	led the French army against England
Mozart:	composed the "Moonlight Sonata"
Nadia Comaneci:	scored the first perfect 10 in Olympic gymnastic competition
Alexander the Great:	conquered the known world
Cameron Crowe:	wrote and directed the movie Jerry Maguire

After you have shared answers, ask students, "**How old were these people when they achieved their success?**"

Let students throw out some guesses if they wish. The correct answers are:

Joan of Arc:	led the French army at 16
Mozart:	composed and performed his first opera when he was 12
Nadia Comaneci:	scored the first gymnastic perfect 10 and won the Olympic gold medal at age 15
Alexander the Great:	began his reign at 20 years of age
Cameron Crowe:	became contributing editor of Rolling Stone when he was 16

Check This . . .

Play Michelle Tumes' song "He's Watching Over You," from her album *Listen* while students work on their sheets.

Materials needed:
Butcher paper and marker or chalkboard and chalk; Bibles

Check This . . .

Show a clip from any movie that depicts the lives of the people on your list. For example, show the scene from *Amadeus* that begins at ten minutes and lasts for one minute showing Mozart, the child prodigy, in action.

Check This . . .

Play the U2 song "I Will Follow," from their *Greatest Hits 1980-1990* album.

Materials needed:
Baby pool; prize; Bibles

Check This . . .

Show the video parable "Stay Dry," from *Shock Wave, Vol 3*. It depicts a kid who plays closer and closer to a swimming pool even though his mother told him specifically not to get wet.

Check This . . .

Play the song "Give Me a Reason," recorded by Third Day on their *Conspiracy No. 5* album.

Once they know how young these people were, read Ecclesiastes 11:9–12:1 aloud to the group. Then, discuss these questions:
- **How old do you have to be to make an impact on the world?**
- **What are the advantages of following God in your youth?**

Comment, **"You probably all know adults who have followed God since their youth and those who turned to the Lord late in their lives. Do their stories agree with Solomon's words? Why or why not?"** Continue by asking:
- **Are you following Solomon's advice? Why or why not?**
- **What happens to the people who follow God in their youth?**
- **What happens to those who don't?**
- **What caution does Solomon give?**
- **How does Solomon challenge us to act?**

LIVING TO TELL

1 A Drop's All It Takes

Place a baby pool filled with water in the middle of your meeting room. To make this illustration more vivid, offer an attractive prize, one that people would be willing to risk getting wet for. Figure out how many people could comfortably fit around the outside of the pool and set that as the maximum number of contestants who will compete.

Then, say something like this: **"We're going to have a competition for this lovely prize. (Announce your prize.) Everyone sitting next to the pool can compete for this prize. The contest is easy: The person who gets the closest to the water and the most of their body over the water without actually getting wet wins. The second you get any water on you, whether from touching it yourself or by being splashed by others, you are out."**

Allow anyone who wants to compete for the prize to circle around the pool. Announce "Go" and let the competition begin. Have someone else help you judge who comes the closest to the water and disqualify anyone who gets wet. If your prize is desirable enough, people should be getting wet and even falling in the pool, hoping to win the prize. After only one dry person remains or no one else wants to attempt getting closer, hand the prize over to the winner, then ask the contestants to answer these questions:
- **How many of you found this game difficult? Why?**
- **Why did you push yourselves closer to the water even though you might get wet?**
- **Do you ever take these kinds of risks in everyday life?**

Ask the contestants to sit down and form groups of four. Instruct them to read Ecclesiastes 12:13, 14. Then, ask them to discuss the following:
- **Have you ever kept getting closer and closer to sin so that you finally "accidentally" fell in?**

- **Since God will judge everything, what should be our attitude toward sin?**
- **How close should you get to it?**

2 Thou Shalt, Ummmm . . .

Show the clip from *Monty Python and the Holy Grail* that begins at 1:12:30 and lasts 1½ minutes. The scene shows some priests reading off the verbose rules handed down by God concerning the use of the "holy hand grenade." Ask the group: **"How many of you feel that God's commands are confusing like the movie clip? Why?"**

Say, **"Ecclesiastes 12:13 says we should 'Fear God and keep his commandments.' Can anyone name all Ten Commandments without looking in the Bible?"**

Let a few students attempt to list off all of the Commandments. If they succeed, congratulate them and continue. If no one can, have the last volunteer read Exodus 20:2-17 aloud to the group. Continue by saying, **"These are God's commands to us. By obeying these things, we will have a joyful life. Are there any commands you do not agree with? Are there any commands you do not understand?"**

Take this time to clarify any of the commands. Especially take time to explain to them in modern terms exactly what taking the Lord's name in vain and coveting means. Finally, distribute writing utensils and copies of the student sheet found on page 55 to each student. Ask students to take a few minutes to complete the sheet. After they have completed their work, ask, **"Which is the hardest commandment to keep? Why?"**

Conclude this session by praying for each other for strength and wisdom in keeping the commandments. Distribute the midweek devotional, **Calculating the Data,** and encourage students to complete the activity this week.

Materials needed:
Bibles; writing utensils; VCR; TV; reproducible student sheets on pages 55, 56 of this book

Skeletons in Your Closet

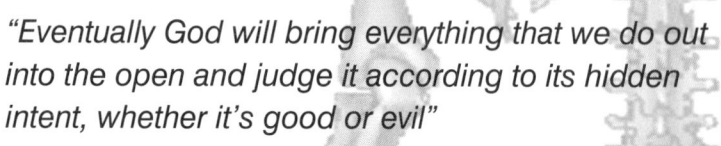

"Eventually God will bring everything that we do out into the open and judge it according to its hidden intent, whether it's good or evil"
                    Ecclesiastes 12:14, *The Message*

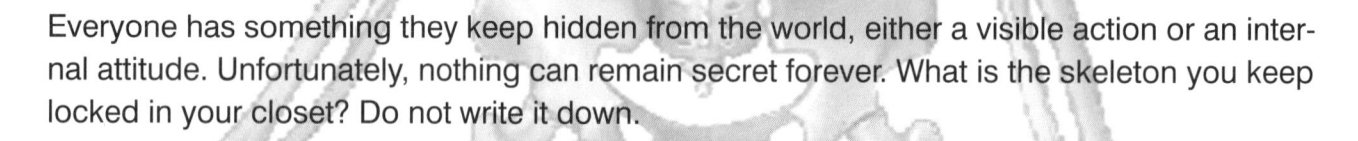

Everyone has something they keep hidden from the world, either a visible action or an internal attitude. Unfortunately, nothing can remain secret forever. What is the skeleton you keep locked in your closet? Do not write it down.

• Why do you keep this skeleton?

• Would you stop if people knew about it?

• List three things you can do to get rid of this skeleton:

1.

2.

3.

Pray for God's strength to clean your skeleton out of your closet. Meditate on Philippians 4:13: *"I can do everything through him who gives me strength."* Seek out someone you trust whom you can confide in (your pastor, a friend, a family member). Share your skeleton with this person and ask him or her to keep you accountable for having a clean closet.

The Ten Commandments Revisited

Fill in the spaces below with the Ten Commandments (Exodus 20:2-17) written in your own words. You cannot change the commands' meaning, only update the language so you will remember them more easily.

1. You shall have no _____ before me.

2. You shall not make for yourself _____, or any _____. You shall not _____ them or _____ them.

3. You shall not _____ the name of the LORD your God, for the LORD will _____.

4. _____ the _____, to keep it holy. Six days you shall _____ but the seventh day you shall _____.

5. _____ your _____ and your _____, that you may _____.

6. You shall not _____.

7. You shall not _____.

8. You shall not _____.

9. You shall not _____ your neighbor.

10. You shall not _____ your _____'s _____, _____ or _____ or anything that _____.

Calculating The Data

"'Teacher, which is the greatest commandment in the Law?' Jesus replied: 'Love the Lord your God with all your heart and with all your soul and with all your mind.' This is the first and greatest commandment. And the second is like it: 'Love your neighbor as yourself.' All the Law and the Prophets hang on these two commandments" (Matthew 22:36-40).

This is God's version of Cliff's Notes for you. His entire law can be summarized in two commands: love God and love your neighbors. Simple, right? If it were, the world would be Utopia. Take the next full day to try and carry out these commands. Meditate on the verses all day and write down all the ways you demonstrated love to God and to your neighbor. (If you want to know who your neighbor is, read Luke 10:25-37.)

Loving God **Loving Neighbors**

Were there any opportunities you missed to love God and others today?

Memorize Matthew 22:36-40 this week and see if your love flows to those around you more easily.

This Is Your Life!
Bonus Session

Throughout the course of this study, your students learned how their lives become meaningless without God in the center, without him directing and focusing all their activities. This gathering provides an opportunity to enjoy themselves and celebrate the life God has given them so far. In addition, this outreach allows them to share, in a non-threatening way, what they learned from Solomon and the inspiration for their lives with their family and friends.

> **Focus**
> The purpose of this special event is to reaffirm to your teens, their friends and families how remembering their Creator in the days of their youth is the key to finding meaning in their lives. As a result of this evening, your students will:
> - Understand how God has affected their lives.
> - See the need to share their life stories with friends and family.
> - Verbalize to others what God has accomplished in them.

Setting Up for the Event

The evening should follow the format of a typical rehearsal dinner for a wedding. Open the doors of your church fellowship room, or possibly rent a room in town to make the gathering less frightening to non-Christians. Ask everyone to dress casually formal to make the evening a special one. You may choose to offer finger foods, drinks and hors d'oeuvres, or you might decide to turn the event into a full-fledged sit-down banquet. A dinner will make the event more memorable, but may prevent people from coming due to cost. It is up to you, but your intent should be to open "This Is Your Life!" to as many people as possible.

Planning the Event

The theme of the night is looking back and celebrating the lives of your students. Each student in the youth group will prepare something to share with everyone at the event. This should retell the most memorable and important event in each of their lives. What makes this presentation unique is how their knowledge of Ecclesiastes will color their stories and convey that life without God is meaningless. Students can choose the exact way they present their stories, tailoring them to their own personalities. Some possibilities are these:
- Simply tell the story.
- Show a videotape of the incident they wish to share (a baseball game, birthday party, school play, etc.)
- Bring pictures or slides that complement their story.
- Reenact their story, using extra actors, sound effects and props.
- Use puppets or action figures to act out the story.

- Recreate the event on video.
- Paint a picture, write a poem or sing a song that describes the story.

Not only can the presentation methods be different, the stories themselves can also take on different tones. They can be:

- **Funny**

   Embarrassing moments, blunders, outrageous situations
- **Heartwarming**

   Sweet moments, cute stories, tearjerkers
- **Suspenseful**

   Dangerous situations, fearful times, brushes with death
- **Heartbreaking**

   Serious illnesses, death, personal tragedies

As your students prepare their presentations, tell them that the only requirement for a successful story is that it connect with an audience. Think of popular movies. The success of a film does not necessarily hinge on its being a comedy, drama or action film, but on whether or not people connect to the movie and care about what happens to the characters. The same applies to the stories of your students. As long as the audience can relate and empathize, it will interest them.

The most important aspect of every story is the central theme that will be carried throughout the night. Each story should reinforce one of two statements:

- **God brought added meaning and light to the situation.**
- **The situation would have been easier if I had looked to God in the midst of it.**

The main thing is to make the presentations interesting. Make sure the stories are told in a variety of ways. An hour of students reading poems will test an audience's constitution like water torture. Keep the presentations to a time limit. Sometimes a microphone can warp students' brains into believing anything they say into it magically becomes interesting, thus taking the stage hostage with a story that would send an insomniac into slumberland. This celebration should remain lively and interesting, because the purpose is to show how exciting and fulfilling life with God is, not how dull, pointless and boring it is.

To accomplish that, it would be a good idea to preview all of your students' presentations beforehand. Before your event, you should run through the entire evening with your students. This will give you the opportunity to work with them on stage presentation. More importantly, it allows you a preview of the material so you can put the performers in the best order possible. It also gives students a chance to perform before an audience and discover any areas that need improvement. Emphasize to your students this dry run is only to make the evening and message more attractive to their audience, not to change what they want to say or evaluate their lives. This will also give you an opportunity to pray corporately for the event. Lift up the nonbelievers to the Lord, asking him for open hearts and minds and the planting of fruitful seeds.

PULLING OFF THE EVENT

First, create a festive, interesting ambiance. Show guests they will enter a time warp after setting foot in the meeting room. Either place some dry ice above the doorways so they must walk "back in time" through the steam, or give them something to wear (such as a badge, bracelet or sticker for their hand) that gives them time-travel abilities. Once inside, they should immediately hear upbeat music. Choose whatever you feel is appropriate to your group, though swing music (by bands such as The W's, Flight 180, Andrew Carlton and the Swing Doctors) might prove the most appealing to all ages.

Ahead of time, you may want to scan into a computer some pictures of your students growing up. Use PowerPoint® to create a slide show that runs continuously while guests arrive, giving everyone something to talk about and break the ice. Finally, if possible, use students' baby pictures as an indicator for where they should sit, similar to a name card at a rehearsal dinner. This will force people to mingle as they must guess who each child is.

On the night of the event, you will serve as emcee. Keep the program light and swift. If possible, get your hands on any baby pictures, videos, stories or other surprises you can throw out about a student's life before his or her presentation. Parents will be more than happy to supply incriminating evidence. (CAUTION: If a student will be mortified or embarrasses easily, wait until after he or she speaks to throw some curve balls. You do not want to throw off their presentations. Refrain from doing anything that might take away from the focus of the entire evening, no matter how funny it is.)

If possible, depending on the number and types of stories, group all of the presenters together by the year in which their stories occurred. This way, you can introduce the section with a few bits of trivia for the corresponding year (such as important national events at the time, sports accomplishments, popular television shows, etc.) You may want to show a few movie clips from that year's popular movies before the first student in each section. You could also play snippets of that particular year's popular songs while students come on and off stage.

The most difficult to accomplish, but possibly the most rewarding aspect of the evening is to secure a mystery guest. Invite a former teacher, staff member or student who meant a great deal to the student ministry in the church. Bring the person back to wrap up the evening, having the guest share a story that involves many of the students in the room and also coincides with the theme of the evening. Budget and availability definitely impact this component, but the right person and story could make the event unforgettable.

The bottom line for the evening is that teens and parents should enjoy themselves and know that life spent staring at the Son is a wonderful life indeed!

ALTERNATE IDEAS

In case your students might not react warmly to the idea of showcasing themselves, try out a few of these ideas:

- **Involve your teens' parents.**

Let them provide the information on their kids by presenting a video photo album, and let them narrate as the pictures are flashed for the audience. They will have insights about their teens' lives that your students don't have about themselves. And, think of the potential of reaching parents who don't have a relationship with Jesus! In the event that a student does not have a parent who would make the presentation, an adult leader could step in with a tribute.

- **Have someone create a videotape.**

A techie adult or teen could video the teens in action over a period of weeks, adding a soundtrack of music and Scripture. The footage would run the gamut from the sublime to the ridiculous. This would be a good way to weave in the references from Ecclesiastes—like 3:1-8.

- **Have your teens create some skits.**

Encourage students to get together and compose some dramatic sketches about their lives, particularly for those who have grown up in the church together. Church photo archives would be helpful here. Students could write "remember when" skits of the times the group did each thing. Ecclesiastes 3:1-8 could provide a framework. For instance, a time for "war" could be mudpit wrestling or a food fight.

- **Create a yearbook.**

Someone who does Creative Memories books would be perfect for this project. Each teen or set of parents could supply a couple of pictures, some memorabilia and some copy, as well as a "life Scripture" or other scriptural insight, for his or her page.

Other EMPOWERED YOUTH PRODUCTS from Standard Publishing

order # 23315
(ISBN 0-7847-1099-6)

WHAT'S THE BIG DEAL ABOUT SEX?
By Jim Burgen

In a national survey of teens, 99% said their number-one concern is how to say no to sexual pressure. Did you know:
- AIDS has been the sixth leading cause of death among 15-24 year olds since 1991?
- Every day 2,700 teens become pregnant?
- Every 24 hours, another 3,000 lose their virginity?
- Of those that become pregnant, more than three in ten choose to abort the baby?

But God has a better way. The *big deal* is that God has an awesome plan for this generation. In a direct, humorous and compelling way the author gives real answers to questions about waiting, dating, homosexuality, interracial dating, dealing with mistakes and more. And each chapter gives readers an opportunity to get personal with questions for reflection. Whether you work with junior-high or senior-high teens, this book will help you deal with this hot topic in a relevant way.

order # 23313
(ISBN 0-7847-0903-3)

FREESTYLIN' A Creative Study of the Book of Galatians
By Bryan Belknap

This six-session resource for junior- and senior-high teens will help your students discover the freedom they have in Christ. This course emphasizes the ability to live by faith, free from sin and fear of the Law. Each session features video clip and music suggestions, reproducible student sheets, a midweek guide for personal devotions and creative learning activities! Also features a bonus outreach game that provides students an opportunity to make real-life application.

STAND YOUR GROUND A Creative Study of the Book of 1st Peter
By Michael Warden

Say no to compromise! This hard-hitting study of 1 Peter challenges students to stop slipping through life with a pseudo-commitment to Christ, one based on convenience rather than conviction. As they choose to be different from the world students may encounter ridicule, persecution & suffering. For Senior high teens. A bonus session helps students discover some ways in which they can help persecuted Christians worldwide.

order # 03397
(ISBN 0-7847-1079-1)

order # 23322
(ISBN 0-7847-1152-6)

RIGHTEOUS ACTS Contemporary Sketches for Youth Ministry
By John Cosper

Relativism, hypocrisy, stress, suicide, violence, forgiveness, loneliness, music and witnessing are hot topics with teens. *Righteous Acts* lights the fires of discussion with dramatic sketches that put these topics at center stage! Sixteen reproducible scripts.

HEARTBURN A Blazing Six-Week Study of the Psalms
By Rick Bundschuh

Psalm 39:3 says, "My heart grew hot within me, and as I meditated, the fire burned." This six-session resource will set senior-high teens ablaze by exploring the breadth and depth of God-centered worship. The package comes complete with a CD featuring red-hot modern Christian music by bands like Spooky Tuesday, Havalina Rail Co., 180 and Soul-Junk. In addition to chord and lyric sheets for all six worship tunes, additional pages feature band photos and bios, thoughts on contemporary worship, reproducible student sheets and a guide for personal devotions.

order # 23316
(ISBN 0-7847-0930-0)

TO ORDER, CONTACT YOUR LOCAL CHRISTIAN BOOKSTORE.
(IF THE BOOK IS OUT OF STOCK, YOU CAN ORDER BY CALLING 1-800-482-2060.)

BOTH BOOKS AVAILABLE NOW

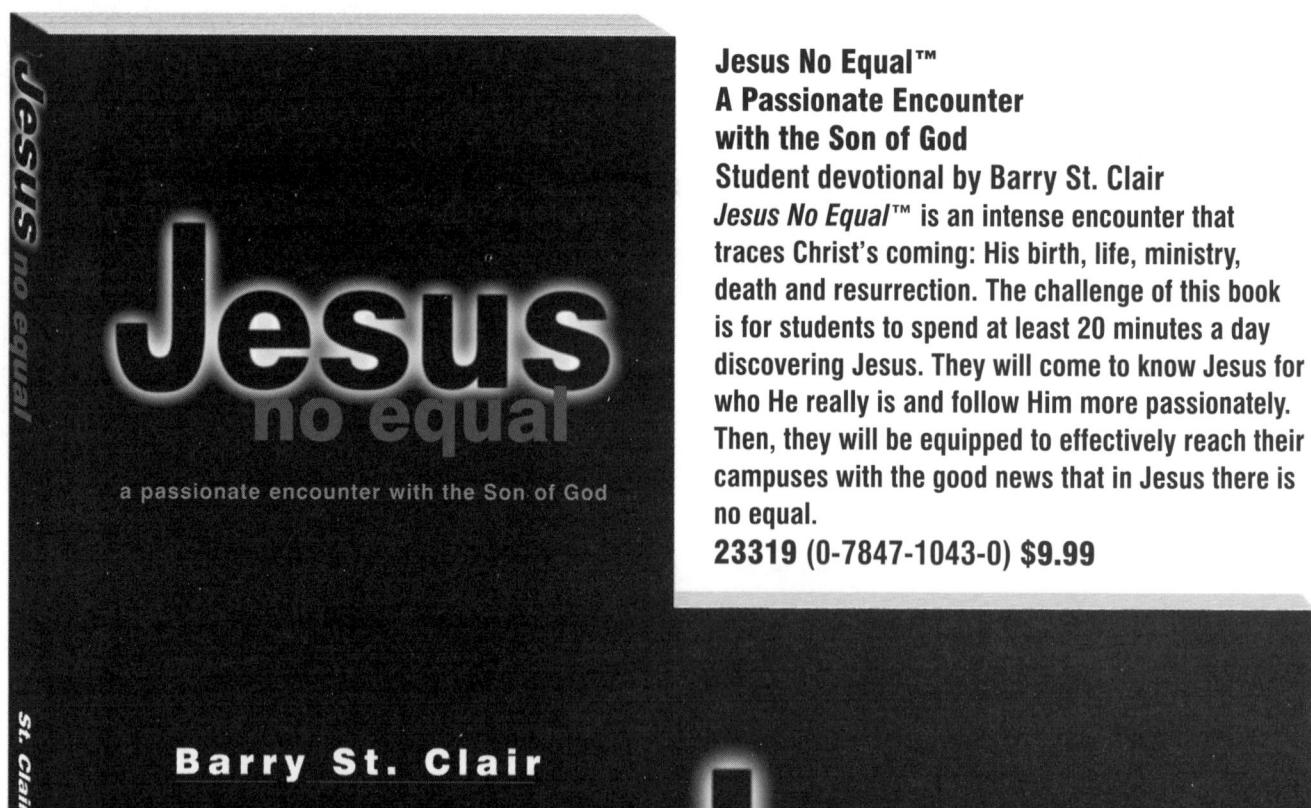

Jesus No Equal™
A Passionate Encounter with the Son of God
Student devotional by Barry St. Clair
Jesus No Equal™ is an intense encounter that traces Christ's coming: His birth, life, ministry, death and resurrection. The challenge of this book is for students to spend at least 20 minutes a day discovering Jesus. They will come to know Jesus for who He really is and follow Him more passionately. Then, they will be equipped to effectively reach their campuses with the good news that in Jesus there is no equal.
23319 (0-7847-1043-0) **$9.99**

Jesus No Equal™
A Passionate Encounter with the Son of God
Leader's guide
by Barry St. Clair & Steve Miller
Leaders can also pave the way for students with the *Jesus No Equal*™ six-session leader's guide that is intended for use with the student devotional. This guide equips youth leaders, student leaders and campus missionaries to effectively reach this generation of students. In addition, the leader's guide features songs from the Sparrow Records compilation, *Listen Louder*. Each session in this book includes a song from one of today's favorite Christian artists.
23320 (0-7847-1042-2) **$7.99**

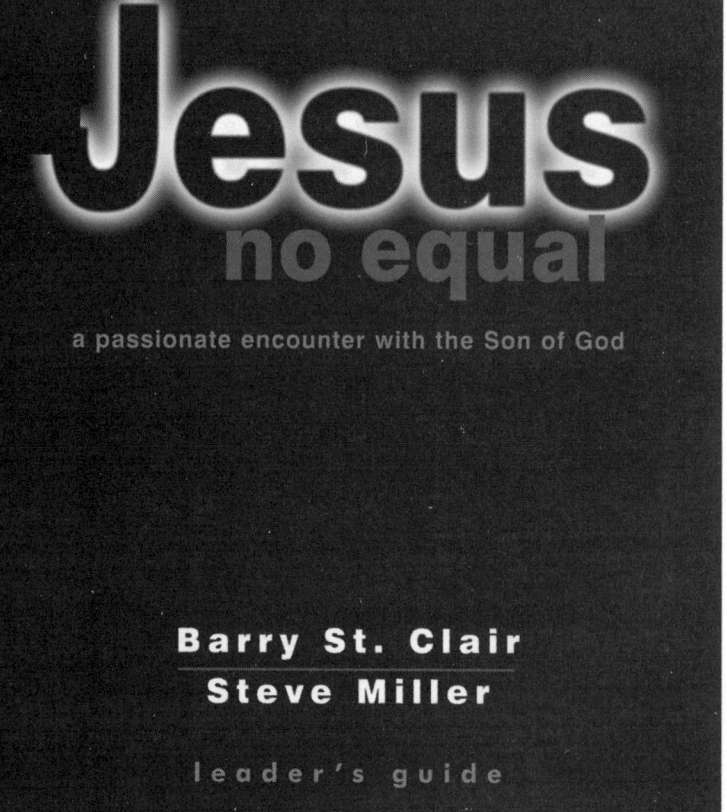